Shaman

... an ever-growing l...

Aubry's Dog, Melusine Draco
A practical and essential guide to using canine magical energies

Black Horse White Horse, Melusine Draco
Feel the power and freedom as Black Horse, White Horse guides you down the magical path of this most noble animal

Celtic Chakras, Elen Sentier
Tread the British native shaman's path, explore the Goddess hidden in the ancient stories; walk the Celtic chakra spiral labyrinth

Druid Shaman, Danu Forest
A practical guide to Celtic shamanism with exercises and techniques as well as traditional lore for exploring the Celtic Otherworld

Elen of the Ways, Elen Sentier
British shamanism has largely been forgotten: the reindeer Goddess of the ancient Boreal forest is shrouded in mystery ... follow her deer-trods to rediscover her old ways

Following the Deer Trods, Elen Sentier
A practical handbook for anyone wanting to begin the old British paths Follows on from *Elen of the Ways*

Trees of the Goddess, Elen Sentier
Work with the trees of the Goddess and the old ways of Britain

Way of the Faery Shaman, Flavia Kate Peters
Your practical insight into Faeries and the elements they engage
to unlock real magic that is waiting to help you

Web of Life, Yvonne Ryves
A new approach to using ancient ways in these contemporary
and often challenging times to weave your life path

What people are saying about

Shaman Pathways – What Is Shamanism?

I recommend this book as a wide-ranging collection of essays
that will be of interest to core shamans and others who want an
overview of this new psychological approach to healing which,
as some of the authors note, has made a huge impact on the
Western imagination in just the last 30 years or so of its existence.
Ross Heaven, author of *Medicine for the Soul* and *Hummingbird's
Journey to God*

Shamanism has often been seen as a complicated practice. This
council of experts in the shamanic field point the reader towards a
clear understanding of this beloved earth centred tradition, whilst
sharing their wisdom, experiences and wealth of knowledge. A
must-read for anyone who is serious about enriching their lives on
many levels.
Barbara Meiklejohn-Free, The Highland Seer

Eleven authentic, insightful essays by established authors and practitioners in the field which discuss a variety of the questions and
issues that are frequently raised about shamanism and animism.
Another useful, delightful book from Moon Books 'Shaman Pathways' series. *What Is Shamanism?* is a compact treasure trove of material providing an excellent source of information and much food
for thought for both practitioners and readers new to shamanism.
June Kent, Editor of Indie Shaman

The collection of articles in *What Is Shamanism?* come from a variety
of contributors with different experiences, backgrounds and opin-
ions. It is an interesting read with a tease for further exploration
about the books they've written.
Katherine Wood, MA, co-author of *The Hidden Worlds*

What Is Shamanism?

SHAMAN PATHWAYS

What Is
Shamanism?

Edited by Trevor Greenfield

MOON
BOOKS

Winchester, UK
Washington, USA

First published by Moon Books, 2018
Moon Books is an imprint of John Hunt Publishing Ltd., No. 3 East Street, Alresford
Hampshire SO24 9EE, UK
office1@jhpbooks.net
www.johnhuntpublishing.com
www.moon-books.net

For distributor details and how to order please visit the 'Ordering' section on our website.

Text copyright: Trevor Greenfield 2017

ISBN: 978 1 78535 802 9
978 1 78535 803 6 (ebook)
Library of Congress Control Number: 2017957122

A CIP catalogue record for this book is available from the British Library.

Design: Stuart Davies

Printed and bound by CPI Group (UK) Ltd, Croydon, CR0 4YY, UK

We operate a distinctive and ethical publishing philosophy in
all areas of our business, from our global network of authors to
production and worldwide distribution.

Contents

Foreword

In a time when we seem increasingly disconnected from the natural world around us, many are finding themselves drawn to shamanism; not necessarily wishing to become a shaman but inspired towards living a shamanic lifestyle, one that is connected to the world as a whole, practically, mentally, emotionally and spiritually.

It can, however, often be difficult to get any conclusive information on what shamanism actually is. This is because defining shamanism is not necessarily simple, nor is it straightforward. All too often you will find on-going debates such as: whether it is possible for anyone who is not a tribal member to practice shamanism; if core shamanism is actually shamanism; whether it is possible for contemporary shamans to be spirit taught, or whether it is even possible for contemporary shamans to exist. These debates can override the need for authors to provide those starting out with real practical examples of what shamanism is – which is where *What Is Shamanism?* comes in and why it has been written.

In this compilation eleven shamanic practitioners share their own perspectives about shamanism. The authors differ from each other in the approach they take, the way they work and how they view shamanism; which is absolutely perfect as it highlights the immutable fact that in shamanism there is really no right or wrong, there is only the way that works for each of us.

None of the authors is trying to tell the reader how to practice shamanism but instead taken as a whole *What Is Shamanism?* provides a well-rounded, although not exhaustive, view of what shamanism is, as of course, for every one of these authors there is another who would have explained it in a different way, from a totally different perspective. Thus is the world of shamanism.

What Is Shamanism? explores the differences between indigenous and modern shamanism, looking beyond cultural appropriation towards authenticity in modern shamanism. In doing this it sheds light on an area that many publications shy away from, that of the Middle World. How shamanism can be an active spiritual practice and ways of working with spiritual entities are also visited along with animism, a key element of all forms of shamanism. Inner soul work is explored along with animals and healing. The compilation ends with a first-hand account of British Shamanism and shamanic story weaving.

It is envisaged that through these writings the reader will find something that resonates with them, that shines light into the darkness of what shamanism is and that through this they may find their own path in shamanism. Often when this happens many discover that they have been working or living shamanically all the time and their fears about what they are doing vanish.

This is an important compilation and one that speaks to the shaman within us all.

Yvonne Ryves author *Shaman Pathways: Web of Life*

What Is Shamanism?

Kenn Day

Stationed at the firelight's periphery, the shaman has, through eons of time, served as shield and intermediary between the community huddled around the fire and the unknown. Shamans still hold this position, but in the modern Western world, the nature of community and the unknown has changed beyond recognition. We no longer live in a tribal culture as a cohesive whole, and the unknown is defined by what little remains that cannot be measured by science. Yet we still peer into the darkness, searching for connections between ourselves and our ancestors, the Earth, and each other. Today, the universal relevance of Shamanism transcends ethnic and cultural boundaries in its applicability for all humanity. The practices of shamanism have found fertile ground even in those who are not called to fulfill the role of shaman, but who still feel the desire to reconnect with so much of what has been lost in our evolutionary sprint toward an ever less spiritual and natural world.

Endemic to shamanic practice is the use of trance states. These allow the practitioner to move at will into the realms of spirits in order to communicate, learn, negotiate, and develop lasting relationships with these beings. This set of practices exists in indigenous tribal cultures around the globe. In these traditional settings, a shaman is defined as one who enters into a trance state and interacts with spirits, either by Journeying to where the spirits are, or by bringing the spirits into their own body, in order to bring information back to the ordinary realm to facilitate change, most often concerning healing and the retrieval of information which forms the practice of spirit divination.

While the definition of a shaman is narrow, the set of practices that can be used in support of shamanic healing and divination is quite varied. Much of it is based upon a fundamental worldview largely forgotten by technological cultures in the modern Western world. Animistic in nature, this orientation views all things as inherently alive, and imbued with the presence of the divine. The highest value is placed on the communal nature of humankind over the individual, recognition of the beneficial presence of ancestors, even after their death, and the repair and maintenance of balance between our human community and the natural world. Ultimately, the view that arises from shamanic practice points to a relationship with self that includes a much larger and more complex sense of soul than that found in monotheistic religions. This broader perspective is essentially transformative, bringing about developmental stage shifts and changing the very nature of identity.

There are three main types of shaman found in active practice today. Indigenous shamans are those who operate within their existing tribal cultures or who have reconstructed an indigenous practice or have been adopted into an existing tribal culture. Core shamanic practitioners base their practices on the work of Michael Harner and his theory that certain universal practices which occur in all shamanic cultures can be lifted out of their tribal context and used by anyone. Post-tribal shamans, are a natural evolution of the indigenous shaman, are chosen and initiated by spirits to serve individuals in the cultures of the modern West.

What separates the role of the shaman from that of lay practitioners is that the work is done in service to others. Just as a doctor requires training and certification before entering practice, a shaman first needs to be recognized by the spirits as having the necessary talent, then they need to receive competent training and, finally, to be initiated by the spirits.

The role of the shaman has always been defined by the needs of their community. Since the most important element of the tribe is the communal whole, the tribal shaman will work to meet the needs of their tribe. It is to this community that the shaman owes their loyalty and their service. For the post-tribal shaman or core shamanic practitioner, serving in our modern, urban environment, this sense of community is made up of whoever uses their services. For them it is the individual who they are focused on serving. This reflects the direction of social evolution in our culture, which values the individual over the communal. However, what defines the shaman in all cases is the nature of his or her work and how he or she relates to community through their service.

This definition is necessary to our understanding of just what shamanism is, so let's break it down.

A shaman is one who moves into a trance state in order to communicate with spirits, to cause changes and/or bring back information, in service to others.

Trance state

A trance state is an altered state of consciousness which allows for movement into the realm of the spirits. This state can be accessed through various means, ranging from simply mental discipline and drumming to extreme physical distress and plant medicines. Most shamans focus on the techniques of sound or movement – drumming, rattling, dancing – to carry them into the altered state. With practice, the shaman is able to drum, chant, dance and communicate with their clients in the physical realm, all while in a trance state. It is important that the shaman is responsible for moving into the trance. It is not something that they fall into without intention. There are some kinds of spirit medium who do this, and this separates them from the disciplines of shamanism.

Communication with spirits

Once they can enter a trance state, the shaman looks for a way to connect with the world of the spirits. This other world is accessed through various doorways, some in the natural world, some within the shaman. Moving through these doorways, the shaman encounters the spirits that inhabit this other world. Often these spirits have an interest in the shaman and his or her community. This provides an excellent starting point to develop a relationship with the spirits. Once rapport is established, relationships can be built. The shaman will usually have one of more special relationships with Spirit Allies. These are special spirits who assist the shaman's work in various ways, sometimes becoming mentors and teachers as well.

Causing change/healing

It wouldn't do anyone much good if the shaman just Journeyed for personal amusement. It is when they do so for their community that it becomes shamanism. One of the most common uses of shamanic Journeying is to bring about healing for another person. In traditional shamanism, this person would be a part of the shaman's clan, tribe, family or village. For those working in a post-tribal setting, the person is most likely a client who has sought them out for their skills. These healings may be for a particular physical illness or for a mental disorder, but more likely there is a soul-level issue that is creating physical and/or psychological symptoms which drop away once the healing is complete.

Bringing back information/divination

The shaman can also serve their community through divination. This is the practice of communicating with the spirits to bring greater and deeper understanding about some aspect of what is being looked at. The shaman may read messages from the spirits in natural phenomena, like cloud formations, the flight of birds or the entrails of slaughtered animals. These days, it is more likely to use a tool like a black mirror, a pendulum, or a set of objects that were found with the help of the shaman's Allies.

Some reconstructionists use runes or cast lots as well. Whatever tools are used, the shaman connects with their spirit helpers, the ancestors of the client or even gods and goddesses to find answers to the questions they are asked. These questions must be of a serious nature, without an apparent method of being answered by ordinary means. Once an answer is received, the one who asked is generally obligated to follow whatever advice they have received.

In service to others

As mentioned above, the shaman works in service to others. In traditional settings, this meant those who shared the same tribe or village, however, for shamans working in the West, this generally refers to anyone who seeks them out for their services. In this way, the shaman still serves community, even as the nature of that community is transformed.

These elements form the fundamentals of shamanic practice. Of course most shamans perform many other functions as well. Shamanic practice will usually include some sort of soul retrieval, along with extraction, ancestor work, and other spiritual healing.

Just as important as this definition is the preparation required for a shaman to function effectively in the role. This preparation is said to begin before birth, in the spirit realm, as the shaman is chosen for this work. The shaman may or may not have a say in this choice at a soul level, but who is and who is not a shaman tends to be set by the time one is born. However, just being chosen is not enough. You still need to know what you are doing. In a tribal setting, the person would receive training from the existing shaman. In the post-tribal culture, we find our training as best we can.

There is no book or workshop that will make someone into a shaman. That said, both books and workshops can provide a foundation of practical training in the techniques necessary to begin practicing shamanism. In most cases, those attending trainings are not planning on becoming shamans, but rather intend to use what they learn to lead a more fulfilling life, with deeper connections to spirit, land, soul and ancestors.

If chosen by the spirits and well trained, a person will be initiated by the spirits as well. This can be a terrifying and overwhelming experience, often culminating in a real or vividly imagined death, followed by the dismemberment of the body, which is eventually reassembled, along with some added bits and pieces from the spirits. After this initiation, the new shaman is ready to begin practicing for others.

For the lay practitioner, no such initiation is necessary, since there will be no need to connect with a spirit ally or collect missing pieces of someone else. Instead, there is a veritable cornucopia of techniques that lies open to anyone with even a modicum of talent and capacity. These are the people who are fueling a renaissance of shamanic practice in the West. It is their hunger for healing, for connection and for a sense of belonging which they recognize as their soul's birthright, which makes these teachings available in the form of books, videos and workshops. This is how the practice of shamanism survives and thrives in its new forms in the world today, even as the tribal forms of shamanism continue to function, providing us with a palpable link to our own shamanic ancestors.

The transformative elements of shamanic practice are deeply effective for those who were raised in the dominant Western culture. Simply moving beyond the confines of the limited ego identity begins to cause developmental shifts which accelerate with deepening practice. This sort of "moving beyond" is all a part of the practice – moving beyond the physical body and the physical realm; moving beyond the ego into soul; moving beyond the individual into the communal self. All of these offer profound opportunities for those living in our post-tribal culture to reconnect with what our ancestors encountered in the experience of being fully human.

It is this insatiable and incorruptible yearning for wholeness that keeps shamanism alive. It is this hunger to connect with both self and other that calls shamans into being. It is this deep and burning thirst for awakening into soul that turns our attention back towards the inner doorways that lead to the realms of the ancestors, the spirits, the goddesses and gods, to the World Tree, to the vast and ever growing Mystery that lies beyond the circle of flickering light cast by what we think we know.

Indigenous and Modern Shamanic Practice

Imelda Almqvist

What do we actually mean by indigenous and modern shamanic practice? Let's start by defining those things and how they might be different.

In the world of shamanism today, generally, a distinction is made between indigenous shamanic cultures and modern forms of shamanic practice in locations where shamanism disappeared (or went underground) for many centuries. This means that there is both research and re-construction work being done in many locations where dominant Western culture (on reflection a rather odd mix of science and Christianity) is viewed as the preferred (*only viable*) worldview and mode of perceiving reality.

All existing civilizations today were preceded by earlier civilizations that practiced shamanism. Yet shamanism has never been a unified global practice. Shamanism is a word that, in modern times, we use to refer to a spiritual belief system that puts the tribe's connection to Spirit (or the spirits) at the very heart of community life. The figure of the shaman plays a key role in this. Operating somewhere between priest, psychologist and medical doctor, he or she offers healing, guidance on spiritual matters, ceremonial and divination work. All shamanic cultures honor the ancestors of their clan. Outside Time the ancestors are consulted on matters of importance to the community. Even the generations as yet unborn are taken into account when decisions are made that affect the larger Web of Life and all living things (please Google Seven Generations – Great Law of the Iroquois to read more).

Shamanism follows the principle of animism: it believes that all things have in-dwelling spirit and that we can contact these spirits and communicate with them. Here, I refer to not just humans or animals, but also trees, plants, mountains, rocks, winds, rivers etc. (And indeed our own computer! If you are having IT problems – tune into the spirit of your computer!)

Civilizations that have preserved an ancient and (relatively) uninterrupted lineage of shamanic/tribal culture until the present time are called Indigenous Cultures. Well-known examples are the Native American peoples or the tribes of the Amazon. There are countless other, less well-known, examples such as Hmong shamanism in Southern China or the Dravidian mountain peoples of India.

In Western Civilization a schism occurred during the period we call the Renaissance (which was followed by the Enlightenment). This was the time when science, as we know it today, became the dominant mode of perceiving and interpreting reality (some key words are investigation, experiment, causality and evidence). Up to this time there was no separation between alchemy and science, between astrology and astronomy, between philosophy and mathematics and so forth. Today we speak of Newtonian Physics, as Isaac Newton is often called the Father of Modern Physics, but actually the great man spent half his time on metaphysical studies and pursuits!

Here, we also need to acknowledge that non-European early civilizations made very significant contributions to our history of science. Think of the Mesopotamians, Ancient Egyptians, Maya and Chinese. Islam also helped preserve ancient knowledge while adding further insights and conclusions.

Summing up this vast subject rather crudely we can say that there has been a scientific (or linear) Western worldview in operation for some centuries now. This dates from a period when great scientific advances and discoveries were made and science, as we know it today, took shape and definition. Europe moved from the magical and profoundly religious worldview of the medieval period (where trees were seen as the thoughts of God and everything/everyone had its place in a larger Divine

Plan) to a more fragmented secular worldview.

In Europe this period was followed by the Inquisition and Witch Trials (between 1450-1750 CE). The US saw witch trials too (think of Salem). There is a well-known principle in the comparative study of religions stating that new (conquering) religions often demonize the old gods and old ways as they introduce a new pantheon. In Europe the Church Fathers of Early Christianity deliberately instilled a deep-rooted fear in people of the old Pagan ways (including folk magic and herbalism). Many (so called) witches were burned at the stake for their healing skills and knowledge of magic.

Today all Western people collectively carry that fear in their/ our ancestral field as we all have ancestors who would have been affected by this (be it on the accused side or on the accuser side, often both!). Roughly, we can say that in the Renaissance period a split occurred between Church and Science which translated into a split that still affects all of us today. This is the split between the workings of the outside world (everyday reality) which is studied and explained through scientific research and our own personal inner world – where our spiritual or religious beliefs live, as well as our intuition. Sadly, we have lost the ancient art of being polymaths! Astronomers revile astrologers and most scientists have no time at all for alchemical principles (which are essentially spiritual principles!).

This is largely (with much local variation!) where Western Culture has been *at* for about five or six centuries. Currently the paradigm and cultural landscape is shifting again: many people no longer feel that mainstream church teachings resonate with them. They are looking for *something else,* for teachings that are in greater alignment with their intuition and innate spirituality. We see many manifestations of this: from the number of people attending courses in shamanism (my inbox is flooding!) to Ayahuasca Tourism in the Amazon. A wealth of (for lack of a better term) New Age books has flooded the market. People are encouraged to release limiting beliefs and to anchor Love and Light in the world etc. Some of those concepts are downright commercial and dubious: "cosmic ordering" being one such example: *if only we ask the right way, the Universe must give us what we want* ... At the opposite end of this scale recent discoveries in particle physics have turned our understanding of the Universe upside down and inside out. Human comprehension of the ultimate nature of reality has made a quantum leap (actually meaning the tiniest of leaps contrary to common usage of that word!).

All spiritual schools worth their salt teach that there cannot be Light without Shadow. This means that any spiritual path is going to confront people with their own shadow and our collective shadow as much as their capacity to feel *love and light*. This surprises many who prefer to think that one can exist without the other. This is one of the many reasons why high quality spiritual teachings are of crucial importance right now. Spirituality is about living an authentic life, questioning every single choice we make, owning our own side of any difficult encounter, being awake to every single mirror the Universe holds up. In shamanism, as in any indigenous world view, there is no separation between inner world and external reality. *They are one and the same!*

More shadowy manifestations of contemporary spiritual seeking are Ayahuasca Tourism (already mentioned) and the related issue of cultural appropriation. Instead of consulting your own ancestors and the spirits of the land that birthed you or host your life today – people think that they can grab a ready-made slice of spirituality from another nation. Indigenous peoples all over the world have suffered greatly at the hands of Westerners imposing another culture with conflicting values. They have lost their land, their teachings and native languages, suffered bloodshed, had their children stolen (think of the Stolen Generation of Aboriginal children in Australia, removed from their parents for enforced adoption by white Western families). Unspeakable trauma remains in the memories and ancestral field of these peoples. Western spiritual tourists arriving on the scene often add insult to injury, and stealing their traditions and ceremonies is not remotely appropriate. (Please see the chapter by Jez Hughes for more about this!)

At this point, on the subject of shamanism today, I need to mention core shamanism. American anthropologist, Michael Harner, became an observer-turned-participant after working with the Jivaro people in Ecuador. They trained him as a shaman. He returned to the US and decided that those shamanic techniques were so life-enhancing (even life-saving) that he bundled together common shamanic techniques from all over the world stripped of their local flavor and identity: e.g., shamanic journeying (or seeking guidance from the spirits), psycho pomp work (death walking), soul retrieval (largely pioneered by Sandra Ingerman), divination and so forth.

On the positive side, this allowed large numbers of Western (spiritually seeking) people to use shamanism (the most ancient form of problem-solving known to mankind) again. This material has (literally!) saved people's lives (some of those being my own clients and students – meaning I am writing this based on first-hand experience).

On the negative side, some people will say that core shamanism is a "made up thing that stands alone from a true tradition with elders and ancestor". I expect that this debate will continue to rage for some time but I will name this shadow. Core shamanism also stands accused of sanitizing things, stripping shamanism of its darker applications (think sorcery and cursing). Personally, I think this is a far more serious concern because any "underbelly" that goes ignored will come to attention sooner or later.

I was asked to write about Modern Shamanism. What remains is my personal view on what modern shamanism is and where contemporary shamanism might be headed (going on my work with children and teenagers).

It is my personal observation (as an international teacher of shamanism) that many (Western) people who feel called to explore shamanism, start off by doing courses in core shamanism as those are often available in their own area. Once they do so, a sacred journey unfolds with many adventures and profound discoveries along the way.

I encourage all my own students to research their ancestral background while they gain basic competence in shamanism. Where were you born? Are or were there people with a gift for healing in your own family tree? Ask around and make the most of talking to elderly relatives alive today. Where are the bones of your ancestors buried? Go on a pilgrimage there. What languages did your (great) grand-parents speak? If they were Norwegian immigrants in the US – perhaps do an evening class in Norwegian language and culture. Do you have non-biological spiritual ancestors (meaning people who shaped your spiritual life)? What did they teach you or introduce you to? Are there people teaching indigenous forms of shamanism that reflect your personal ancestral blend of influences? Hook up with those teachers. Visit small museums in your area of birth. Search the internet for obscure documents people may have published about research they have done in the same geo-spiritual area ...

For me personally, the ancestors and spirits of place are calling loudly. Around my fortieth birthday, the spirits came one night and pinned me down, demanding that I train as a shamanic practitioner as that was a soul commitment I had made before birth (but had forgotten). I had my hands full with three children aged seven and under, but from reading anthropology books I knew that when the spirits call you to this path, you do not risk death or injury by ignoring them! I did a practitioner training in core shamanism in the UK. In terms of distance this was just about manageable. Going off to Mongolia or Peru for a prolonged period was out of the question and anyway those are not my ancestral lands, I am a Northern European person.

I am Dutch but married to a Swede. Our three children have dual nationality. We divide our time between Sweden and the UK. On my first ever visit to Sweden, aged 19, the Norse Gods seized me. Having been raised as a Roman Catholic this revelation brought on a major shift in my internal world. I was building a close relationship with the Norse gods for fully two decades before I undertook formal training in shamanism. I just did not think of this as shamanism but as a solitary path that chose me *(no one chooses shamanism – shamanism tends to choose us!)*.

It has taken me a while to sort out how training in core shamanism sits with that older pagan and indigenous Northern European tradition in my own life. It is not uncommon to combine the two: many people work within core shamanism as well as their ancestral indigenous tradition (e.g., Sami, Mongolian, Greek, Native American, Zulu Sangoma, West Coast Canadian etc. I am thinking of friends and colleagues typing this!).

As well as speaking about Modern Shamanism, we also need to mention the future of contemporary shamanism: what might be taking shape?

I am teaching some especially gifted groups of (adult) students at the moment (in both Europe and in the US) and, with my encouragement, they have all embarked on epic quests and journeys of ancestral discovery. I adore hearing about their discoveries and the way their own helping spirits and ancestors come forward to guide them and "take them home" spiritually speaking.

On a global level there are wonderful bodies such as The International Council of Thirteen Indigenous Grandmothers who share indigenous teachings and take the role of true Elders of our global community. Theirs are the voices that speak for the preservation of our planet and preservation of indigenous wisdom and ways of life.

All over the world many people are working hard to re-discover and reconstruct the wisdom traditions of their ancestors. A lot of work is done, for instance, in the Northern Pagan Tradition but also the Celtic Tradition and Mediterranean traditions (and that is just Europe!).

An important point I need to make here is that the methods of core shamanism can be used to contact our ancestors and retrieve information. In shamanism we work Outside Time, meaning that nothing is ever truly lost. It can be retrieved or contacted in the Other World, the Spirit World. For that reason I have observed people use core shamanism to reconstruct the faith and medicine of their ancestors and it is beautiful!

Then again, wherever reconstruction occurs differences of opinion are going to occur as well. Some people are hard core, they would prefer to go and live in eleventh-century Scandinavia as Vikings. Others feel that any tradition can only stay alive by evolving and adjusting to modern times. *(My personal take on this is that gods and goddesses wish to evolve along with us, through interaction with human beings. I do not perceive them as static or frozen entities. Others will disagree with that!)*

Just as Christianity has fragmented into different churches with different ideologies there is strong potential for such endeavors to fragment too and create opposing camps arguing and bad-mouthing each other. In part, this is the human condition: we define ourselves by what we are and what we are not ("us and them"). As the human race evolves (I remain an optimist despite much evidence to the contrary!) we must learn to heal and dissolve separation – not to add to our divided world full of conflicts and religious-political tensions. This is a work in progress. All of us, individually, are a work in progress!

My own students are demonstrating a raw but phenomenal commitment to their spiritual path at the moment. They are doing things that I have not seen done before. Students from very different ethnic backgrounds are working together, in committed and unified circles. It makes my heart sing to witness this! To be part of this revival of a spirit-led way of life, honoring all sentient beings and larger Web of Life (in Norse shamanism we say Web of Wyrd!).

Actually, the word *indigenous* is a bit problematic because, at the end of the day, *we are all indigenous* – we are all from somewhere! But many of us have lost our tribe, the sense of community and unified cosmology that the indigenous way of life brings. Then again, due to modern communications (internet, iphones, ebooks) people alive today have greater access to information and global connections than any generation before us (who needed to board a ship and sail across oceans guided by the stars to achieve this!).

This takes me to the final section of this chapter. There is another large group of world citizens I have not yet mentioned specifically: young people. Our children and teenagers demonstrate immense and innate spiritual wisdom, given half a chance. The blood of our ancestors runs through them too. Many of them attend schools of wondrous cultural diversity. As a parent of three such teenagers (and as the author of *Natural Born Shamans*) I just wish to say that the young people I work with have already changed the game again. One example: rather than performing core shamanism-style *journeying* they stay attuned to spirit in every moment. They are very fast. They have already seen and grasped the guidance from spirit long before any adult started drumming. They care passionately about the world they inhabit and will inherit.

As a shamanic teacher working with young people (and really they teach me far more than I could ever teach them), I know that we need to trust young people to define their own spiritual practices. Not indoctrinate them in established belief systems but educate them in an open-minded way (and be willing to be educated in return).

For all of those reasons, I personally believe that the

shamanism of the future (be it indigenous or contemporary/ neo/reconstructionist) will be something *new and fresh* that still reflects the key principles many people honor today.

We are all indigenous (as in from somewhere) and we are all world citizens too. We all have ancestors who would have practiced shamanism – therefore shamanism is our birth right!

Shamanism as an Active Spiritual Practice

Dorothy Abrams

A few years ago I had a long challenging conversation with a Native American shaman who enlisted two of my students in her group. She wanted to know if I called myself a shaman and was I willing to take on the ailments of my people in exchange for their healing. I don't and I am not. Nevertheless, I am dedicated to my friends who journey under the drum and work hard for their well-being as I hope they work for mine. We are serious trekkers on the shamanic path which is our active spiritual practice. I call myself a shamanic practitioner and have been known to be critical of recreational shamanism. I expect great things of the people I journey with and miracles from the spirits. Let me explain.

The practice of shamanism in all its various adventures and challenges can take people through an exciting adrenaline rush. People sign up for classes or attend drum circle for the surprising quests their guides assign them. Like an action-packed adventure movie hero, they find themselves chased, rescued, dismembered, confronted and repackaged. They see worlds they never dreamed of and travel through time. Let's face it; if we learn the art of shamanic journey even without psychoactive substances, the world alters itself around us in ways right out of a science fiction fantasy. Or it can.

Those travels are intended to have long-lasting effects. They are deep soul lessons that apply across all of one's lives and bodies. Emotional lessons, physical truths, psychological expansion, and spiritual transcendence are valuable outcomes of taking these immense journeys. However, if one is not sufficiently grounded; if one has no long-range vision, the experiences are forgotten. The spiritual memories are left to work on the unconscious.

The journeys must repeat themselves until the soul recognizes the road traveled. The recreational shaman gets beat up by the process. As we have all said many times, *you do the rituals or the rituals do you.* It is better to do the rituals intentionally and keep good notes.

When we embrace shamanism as our active spiritual practice we center ourselves in this extraordinary energy permanently. Or as permanently as we can. Humans have a nasty habit of becoming distracted. The good news is we can always come back to center and continue on course with perhaps minor corrections. What does that look like – to have an active practice every day and in our dreams?

First, we begin each day with an intentional grounding meditation. This practice may include the dance of the seven directions, the sun salutation, drumming and chanting or a silent meditation in which we draw from Mother Earth and Father Sky through our bodies and connect them to each other. We then proceed through our work-a-day world grounded and centered.

In addition, we maintain daily communication with our spirit guides and animal allies. We are conscious of them riding in the car with us when we are about to make a wrong turn or an accident is averted. We look at a cloud formation and see a message from the animals we partner with. The clouds fly across the sky and point at a hill or river for us to hear. Clouds fly apart in a particular manner to show us what to release and how.

Similarly, a flock of birds whirls and twists together without harm and then separates. Birds fly in different directions. We ask what is forming, re-forming and dissolving. Then we know the answer. A single bird lands on our parked car and pecks at the door insulation trying to get in. Its persistent and odd behavior sends us researching the goldfinch. That in turn connects us with a spirit guide sometimes known as an archangel in other traditions. He wants us to apply our knowledge of soul transcendence and magic to current events. A blue heron sits hunched over on a tree shedding the rain as we drive by on the way to the airport. He is our healing and travel guide. We know we will fly safely even if there are airport terrorist alerts and we were concerned. Just keep our heads down and let the fears of others wash over us. Nothing bad will happen today.

A decision is required about money or property. I know my spirit ally has a larger perspective so I ask, *Should I?* Perhaps they appear in my mind's eye and wordlessly nod or shake their head. The yea or nay is clear. Maybe someone at a nearby table in the pub shouts *Yes!* as they watch the game over the bar. Maybe Amy Winehouse comes on the radio singing *No no no* to *Rehab*, but I know it's about me not Amy Winehouse and the message isn't about rehab. I am not investing time or money today.

Sometimes we miss the obvious answers and need to use shamanic divination. One of those might be a rock reading. With a willing rock we trance until images form on four of its sides. This is magic like a crystal ball. Each carries a piece of the message. Slowly the narrative comes together until we have direct advice from the rock people. When we return to ordinary reality and look at the rock, we wonder where those images are. They are no longer evident in the uneven surface of the stone though they were as plain as day a moment ago.

Another possibility is found in the sound of the drum. Playing the frame drum and listening to its voice, we find our answer in the reverberations. A simple drum beat sings like Tibetan bowls when our thoughts turn to the correct choice. The drum goes flat when we focus on the opposite. If we prefer burning sage and candles on a given day, we watch the smoke rise and turn in unusual shapes. The candle flame dances without air currents. It divides or dies, leaps up or splits. It flickers and dances with the drum. The message is clear because we asked the question and then know the answer.

We can journey to the upper or lower worlds on the question and wisdom we seek. Going deeper with the drum gives us a trance journey to an actual place where we see the outcome of our choices. *Which should I pick?* Only one turns out right. Pitfalls arise elsewhere which are clear in the trance. But another day we are on the bus and cannot drum. We don't even want to close our eyes to journey so we ask our shamanic body, *Should I stay or should I go.* Right is yes. Left is no. We wait and feel the internal pull to the correct decision. It's our guide tugging on our guts or heartstrings. We believe him. Based on long experience we trust and decide *No, let's not make a move.* Less than a month later, the results are in. We missed losing money and entering total chaos that arose from a yes.

Living in partnership with the guides gives us a sense of security in making decisions. These experiences lead naturally to a life of gratitude. We can scarcely receive rescue, advice and warnings without speaking our thanks. I wasn't brought up that way nor were you, I'm sure. But what else is appropriate? Native Americans leave gifts of sacred tobacco and corn pollen as appreciative offerings. Wine or coffee poured on the ground as a libation may be better suited to some guides. A handful of oats thrown to the wind for a horse ally, sage burned in a bowl for a Southwest American Indian drumming guide, a bonfire of the right sacred woods for an old European healer-spirit all speak in symbolic language our spirit allies understand. *This is for you, sir. With my love dear madam.* We need to appreciate the aid they bring with word and deed that suits them.

How do we know what to give? Ask. Simple as that. The shamanic practice is a communicative interchange. We go into a journey and ask what they want. They reply verbally, in images and metaphor or with demonstrations. Our thanksgivings might be shamanic rituals. We are asked to construct a giving altar with items they require like sage, eucalyptus, oats, cornmeal, coins or crystals on the table. We sing their favorite songs or drum for them and listen to the drum horse sing. We burn candles and incense. We make them beautiful pictures with our arrangements or bring flowers to the altar. We dance. In the acts of giving thanks we learn more about how the worlds connect and merge and how consciousness creates our experiences. It's rarely just a party with the spirits.

Sometimes our thankfulness extends to a quest for someone else. We may be told to go to a certain place and create a visual display like stones stacked together at the lake shore or ribbons tied on a magic tree in order to declare our gratitude. Observers understand them according to their own inner truths. We may be asked to erect a display of prayer flags representing the things for which we are thankful. We paint, draw or batik cloth talismans so we can dwell on how deep that act from the guides infused our lives as we make the flags. We continue the gratitude when people ask us about the process and learn of our own inner life. Or we may know someone with a need for healing, food, transportation, or teaching and we volunteer to meet that need in the name of our allies. Being deeply touched by the guides encourages us to love and touch other souls, passing the gifts from spirit on to other humans.

Taking that a step farther, the guides may ask us to become activists for their corner of the Earth. If an animal guide needs wide open spaces, clean air and water, then we find allies among the environmental activists and protect the Earth spaces sacred to our guides. As we are able, we support the organizations positioned to do as much good as possible in this area. We help animal rescue programs with time and money, to rescue moon bears or protect the wolves. We tell people about organizations like Animals Asia and The Wolf Conservation Center which are new to them.

Over the course of time, we increase our human connections to create a drum circle around us and build a tribe. Teaching others is its own spiritual practice. Sharing the basics of how to journey, how to find a spirit guide and animal ally and how to set up shamanic healing circles strengthens our own inner core of shamanic experience. Teaching is a well-worn path for the teacher to learn deeper truths. The planning and preparation draws us closer to the spirits before the class ever happens.

When we draw in experienced journeyers to our circles, the group is able to soar together traveling across the worlds on the same journey to the same place in the lower or upper worlds. Tracking each other builds advanced skills in shamanic rescue and monitoring. A responsible teacher will be able to go out into the other worlds and bring back a friend who is stuck or has strayed. A group able to work together in joint consciousness develops strong healing and prophetic abilities. They can work protection for the Earth and intercession for her people. At times of natural disasters they can journey to assist the dead in finding their way home. Some of these shamanic workings are not ones we would prepare alone. We rely on the synergy of the circle to empower us in making bold interventions that change the course of a soul's journey. Sometimes that involves soul retrievals for fragmented personalities. All of these journeys are service to the tribe, to the larger community and to the Earth.

Sometimes we are asked to perform journeys of service for our guides and animals. They are not omniscient nor invincible. They can grow weary or ill. They can be abducted or imprisoned. They can lose heart, especially if we have not been around them for a while. I had a mischievous acquaintance who thought it amusing to journey and capture my key animal guide. I had no idea he would betray my trust in that manner. Imagine my dismay when I heard the animal's distress call from far far away. I tracked him and released him, unwilling to take retribution for the offense. My guides were not so hesitant. They took the man's rabbit and drowned it as we scurried along the path home. I was shocked. Yet, it is true the guides are not our projections nor thought forms. They have independent existence and free will.

We also are called to perform service to the tribe. Healing each other in drum circle is a common practice. Taking joint journeys on behalf of one member, their relative or a person who has asked is a privilege. The spirit canoe and the heron flight are my favorite group healing journeys. Each one has a lead drummer who guides the direction of the journey from the front of the formation. Others align themselves within the body of the vehicle. Another principle drummer takes hold of the rear and monitors the process. All journey and bring back wisdom which is offered aloud, blown into the body of the ailing, or shared with laying on of hands. The integrity of the process relies on all the travelers being in communion with their guides and working apart from ego.

Sometimes the service involves communication with wind, storm or physical elements. Those who live in shamanic awareness can call the rain, draw a light cooling breeze to the garden or protect a specific place from natural disasters. I learned this directly from my guides who awoke me from a deep sleep immediately prior to a severe thunder storm. They provided a chant of protection to sing three times. Then the storm hit, blew apart a nearby electric transformer and left our house and trees intact. Subsequently, major storms which leveled the neighbors' trees passed over us because the charm was set in place. When to use this skill is a sensitive matter. Simply turning the wind without regard for its next path can be harmful. We don't perform interventions with the forces of nature because we can. We do so when it is clear we must.

How do we know when we must? We wait for that internal tug from the guides. We seek confirmation from one of the divinatory practices if we have time. We journey out on the singing drum to see what the best advice is. Then we trust ourselves and people in the active practice of shamanism to know what is the right and mighty thing to do. At that, it becomes a Nike moment. Just do it.

Any shamanic skill requires that we work in a grounded state, connected to the earth and sky. We perform these miracles in the power of the spirits, not out of our own physical energy. In that way we protect our health and mental prowess. Frankly, the energies called on during shamanic intervention are strong enough to fragment an ungrounded soul, thus creating a new problem for another practitioner to correct. When working as a grounded spirit channel, the actual shift is created by the guides. We are protected from backfires that could harm us. We are shielded from retaliation sent by people who had a stake in maintaining the negative status quo. And we are healed by their therapeutic energies speeding through us. This connection builds a mature active shamanic practice that is more than a coat we put on for the occasional public event. It is who we are.

Working with Spiritual Entities

Janet Gale

Stated simply, shamanic practices are all about working with and for spiritual entities.

The shamanic practitioner is working closely with his or her own helping spirits: non-physical allies with whom he has created a deep connection. This depth of connection and communication assists the practitioner in obtaining insights into the healing medicine required for those persons with whom he is working. Her own personal work and practices have established contact with these helpers, and throughout her healing career and robust personal practice she has deepened and expanded the connection with these unseen beings.

For students and initiates in the introductory phases of shamanic teachings, the first instructions pertain to journeying. A shamanic journey is a type of meditation using a drum, rattle or some other repetitive sound (including the human voice) to shift brainwaves from an alpha state to a theta state. This shift of consciousness opens the gateway to the spirit realm, often referred to as non-ordinary reality. Using intention and an ongoing practice of shamanic journeying, the student is introduced to their own personal guides and teachers, who reside in this altered reality. In these early days of learning, practitioners establish loving and deep relationships with their spirit allies, and, through their guidance, have embarked on many wondrous and exciting insights and awareness into their own healing and spiritual growth.

Throughout the course of the practitioner's life, several initiations take him deeply into the healing work, and with clear intention and compassion, he will begin to work with others to assist in their healing. When we enlist our spirit allies to assist us in helping others, we are endeavoring to "inspire" the client to allow and receive spiritual help. The word inspire is derived from Latin meaning to breathe, or to breathe in spirit. The Wisdom of Solomon 15:11 states: "… inspired into him an active soul." The inference here is that the practitioner, with his non-physical helpers, will be enlivening the spirit of the client. The practitioner knows, if she is truly in her own integrity, that it is not her "doing" the work on the client. As practitioners, we are merely facilitators: being the hands of Spirit, if you will, and it is these helping spirits that can offer the most appropriate healing for the client. The practitioner's spirit allies work closely with the allies of the client. The practitioner is effective only to the extent that she will listen, share, and act on the guidance being offered by these helping spiritual entities. The effectiveness of the practitioner is often measured by how purely they will "channel" the guidance and inspire the client to follow through with the advice and/or healing protocol of the spirit helpers.

The clients have their own spirit allies. One of the causes of dis-ease that has been identified by shamanic practices is the dissociation or disconnection from these spirit allies. In the modern world, we may have become disconnected from nature's spirits and the natural rhythms of the Earth, resulting in feeling separate from others, alone and powerless. A psychological phenomenon coined Nature Deficit Disorder has finally been recognized and accepted by Western medicine. Books and scholarly articles have surfaced describing the results of our increased reluctance to being out of doors. These articles confirm that this disorder may cause significant behavioral issues in children, and may even contribute to an underlying cause of ADD and/or ADHD. As we grow up, our spirits, left untreated by Western medicine, leave us feeling more and more lost. We experience loneliness and unworthiness, and feel powerless in a busy and chaotic world. In shamanic terms, this dissociation is coined as Power Loss.

To address power loss, a practitioner will confer with their spirit allies in an initial diagnostic journey for the client, during which guidance will be given in terms of a course of action. One of the first inroads has generally been to restore the connections with the client's helping spirits – reuniting them with a long lost power animal or non-physical guide. The practitioner will be directed in a process called Power Animal Retrieval for their client.

The spirit ally, who may take the form of an animal, ancestor, ascended master, or even a magical being will be reunited with the client. Some level of understanding by the client will define the form that this entity takes. In other words, the spirit ally will take a form that will make sense to the person receiving it. Perhaps they had a favorite Teddy bear as a child, and the return of a bear ally makes them feel comforted and safe. Perhaps the client has had an encounter with a horse or dog or cat, and one of those animal forms inspires them to feel more courageous and strong. Perhaps the watchful eye of a grandparent who has crossed over will remind the client that they are loved and cared for by the unseen. The return of a unicorn or dragon may inspire the client to trust again in magic or miracle. Whatever healing gift is required, Spirit will provide the perfect bearer of the medicine in spirit form.

Once reunited with their powerful ally, the client can confer and deepen their relationship and continue on their own healing path with a renewed sense of empowerment. In most cases, their sense of belonging in the world, and trust in the support of the Universe is restored. They no longer feel alone.

The client is generally guided to bring more ritual and ceremony into their life. Again, through our disconnection with the natural rhythms of life, we have also fallen away from our ancestral practices, whereby we celebrated the changes in season, the cycles of the moon, the miracles of birth and death, etc. Each season has a spirit, as do all our planetary bodies, and by effectively ignoring our spiritual connection, we have drifted into a state of separation and dis-ease. Ritual and ceremony recognizes our spirit and feeds the spiritual body, which allows us to reconnect with our true selves. That reconnection allows healing to incredible depths!

The practitioner will typically team up with different allies for different types of work. As mentioned, Spiritual Entities take a form that helps us understand the messages that they are offering. In Shamanic practices, they will usually indicate the nature of the work required. For example, I conspire with different allies for soul retrieval than for extraction work. I know as soon as I begin journeying for my client that if certain members of my team arrive, we will be doing a specific type of work together. The practitioner really must be very present and open during every session, and not make his or her own assumptions about what will be required. Spirit is truly doing the work, and the practitioner is to listen and take the appropriate action as directed. If the practitioner's ego steps in, the connection with Spirit is lessened, and the egoic filters of the practitioner taint the information and medicine that Spirit has offered for the client.

According to indigenous peoples, all things are spirit. The trees, the rocks, the sun, the earth, the water, the land, etc., etc., all have and are their own unique spirit. This is where the phrase "all my relations" is probably derived. All spirit is equal, connected and compassionately supported. The practitioner may avail on any of these aforementioned spirit helpers to assist in client work. Also, it is not outside the realm of possibility for any of these spiritual beings to require assistance or healing for themselves. For example, the land affected by a natural disaster may require a restoration of wholeness through ritual or ceremony. The practitioner would connect with the Spirit of the Land and listen to his own Guidance regarding the ritual or ceremony required to restore wholeness in that land. The spirit of a storm might reveal itself to a client that resonates with finding peace within the eye of the storm. There are limitless possibilities within the spirit realm. There are also limitless resources with which to consult!

Within the healing modality of shamanism, there is a second reason that we might not feel well: spiritual intrusion. This is a phenomenon wherein the client has taken on energy that does not belong to him. This energy is misplaced, and has been transferred and accepted into the being of a host. Here we have yet another spiritual entity, which may be as seemingly innocuous as the result of an insect bite, or as overt as a full-blown possession. Possession may look very frightening; changing the personality of a loved one, or initiating a psychotic event. Where a localized "mass" of energy, like an insect bite or pain in a certain area of the body might require the practitioner to perform an extraction to remove the entity, the possessed person would require a much deeper removal, known in shamanism as depossession. The possessing spirit may not realize that it is residing within another living being, and has lost its way. The presence of this spirit can significantly influence the behavior, choices and quality of life in the host. The work of assisting misplaced spirits on their journey home is known as psychopomping.

Here the practitioner is required to interact with his or her own helping spirits to support the possessing entity in returning home. A connection is required to negotiate with and understand the possessing entity, all the while being diligent that the entity does not move from the current host to the practitioner, or to some unsuspecting third party. The practitioner must be careful to hold a robust container for the work, while the helping spirits conspire to do what is best for all involved. Negotiations with the possessing spirit must consider the cosmology of the entity: to send it to the "home" that aligns with their belief system. As you can imagine, this can become quite an involved process that necessitates a practitioner to possess a high level of knowledge, superb connection with Spirit and incredible patience to see the process through to its conclusion. The practitioner must be highly trained in setting their own boundaries of protection, as often the possessing spirit can be quite fearful and confused, requiring great compassion and diligence on behalf of the practitioner.

Misplaced energy and spirits are not limited to attaching themselves to or inhabiting people, but may take up residence in buildings, bodies of water, land, caves, and the like. Energy is not restricted by time and space, and can navigate through either with incredible ease. It is not governed by our earthly rules.

When we are building our homes, we rarely perform blessings, rituals or ceremonies in our modern world, as our ancestors did. Most of us would not think to consult the spirits of the land to ask permission to build our house. We just build on a predetermined place, conforming to local planning commissions and land usage guidelines. During the building process, indigenous people would put offerings and blessings in the foundation and walls. That rarely happens today. In working with the spirits of ancestors, I have often been surprised by their lack of understanding of our modern ways. It is regarded that we have forgotten to honor spirit. There are many aspects of our modern lifestyle that dismiss the importance of spirit in our lives, thinking that we are doing everything on our own. As I understand (and remember) more and more about honoring my own spirit and its connection to all beings, I recognize the need for ceremony to strengthen, restore and nurture my own spirit. If we are not willing to honor and strengthen our own spirit, the spirit of the homes in which we reside, the buildings in which we work, and the land on which we live, how can we possibly begin to understand that all these beings feed and support each other in such positive ways?

In the case of a misplaced spirit inhabiting a building or other physical location, a shamanic practitioner may be called in. He will be required to assess the situation and journey to his helping spirits to seek a peaceful and loving resolution. In most of these types of cases, I have been directed to work with the spirit of the building, the spirit of the water, land, etc., as well as the intruding spirit. In other words, I am working with my spirit allies as a shamanic practitioner, and my allies are then working with the spirit of the "host" and the spirit of the misplaced energy altogether to find a solution. Of course, again, the practitioner is working with spirits, as all things have and are spirits. These spirits are intelligent and have needs to be met. I am always intrigued by these types of sessions, as, from the outside, one may not realize that the building has a spirit that needs to be consulted. Some observers have been quite surprised at the depth of work required to hold these "meetings of spirit" so that a successful, healthy and loving result can be obtained.

The third reason that we might feel disease in our being is a shamanic phenomenon known as soul loss. In the instance of soul loss, a piece of the client's essence has left this reality and resides in non-ordinary reality. When these soul parts are ready to return, bringing with them incredible gifts of healing and a sense of revitalized wholeness, the practitioner carries the essence back from non-ordinary reality and blows it into the heart and crown chakra of the client. In other words, the practitioner literally blows healed spiritual essence into a client to remind them of their wholeness and offer deep healing.

There are multiple spirits that play a part in every session and/or ritual or ceremony. For example, when doing fire ceremonies, the practitioner is working not only with his or her helping spirits, but also intimately with the spirit of the fire. This holds true with all the elements: air, water, earth and of course, fire. To illustrate further that "all beings are our relations," consider that we hold the spirit of these elements within our own beings: The spirit of air is our breath; water is in every cell of our body and also as a metaphor as in the rivers of blood running within us. Earth spirit resides as our bones and the spirit of fire is in our heart. This, to me, clearly shows that we are very connected to spirit on many levels, and are truly united in oneness to all beings. We all have a deep and profound connection with Spirit.

All this to illustrate that shamanic practitioners are all about working with spiritual entities! With the intention of the client and practitioner creating a focus for the work, spirit sets about to create healing. Spirit follows through with a specific intention set, to inspire healing in an individual, a location, a community and/or our planet. We truly are working outside of time and space, conspiring with Spirit to assist ourselves and others in living meaningful, healthy and fulfilling lives. And what are we filling with meaning? Our spirits.

Shamanism and Animism

Laura Perry

Shamanism and animism are two terms that get tossed around a lot these days in discussions about spirituality and religion. They're closely related concepts, almost two sides of the same coin. Or perhaps we might view them, in one sense, as theory (animism) and practice (shamanism). The concepts behind both of these words go back many millennia and can be found in a wide variety of cultures around the world. But they're not always clearly defined, and the distinction between the two can be confusing. Let's see if we can sort them out and discover why they're so important to each other, and especially, why animism is one of the basic underlying components of shamanic practice.

My dictionary defines animism as "the attribution of a living soul to inanimate objects and natural phenomena." Right there, we can see that the definition is written from the point of view of someone who isn't an animist, which is the case with many people in the modern world. Modern society tells us that there is a separation between humans and nature, between us and other animals (yes, we're animals!) and most definitely between us and "inanimate objects." Animism tells us, instead, that we're all connected, all inspirited, all alive and important and sacred.

To an animist, "things" like rocks and trees are indeed alive and are not inanimate objects, or at least, that's not all there is to them. More to the point, animism tells us that we live in a spirit-filled world. Spirits are all around us and, of course, they're within us as well: our own souls. This is the layer of connection, the level at which we're all linked together with the very fabric of the universe, which, in the animistic view, is itself alive.

Some religions insist that the only beings who have souls or spirits are humans. Others will allow that animals might also have souls or spirits. But the animist worldview says that everything is imbued with spirit: every rock, every blade of grass, every star in the night sky, the whole cosmos. And yes, even man-made objects like your phone and your toothbrush have, on some level, a spirit – or at least, they can have a spirit, or be imbued with one. We'll explore the idea of drawing a spirit into created objects later on, since this is an important facet of shamanic practice. But for now, let's look at animism as a worldview, how it works and what it means.

Animism in and of itself isn't a religion or a spiritual path. Instead, it's a worldview or a school of thought that informs and underlies many different spiritual traditions. It appears in varying forms from culture to culture, from Japanese Shinto to the Australian Aborigines to the Tapirapé of the Brazilian rainforest. It's the underlying concept behind many different kinds of Paganism and polytheism, both ancient and modern. Though it's not a terribly common worldview these days, animism is gaining ground as people begin to reconnect with nature and view it as alive and sacred rather than an inanimate resource to be exploited.

It's possible that animism is the oldest way humans have of looking at the universe and interacting with it. And ultimately, what it says is that we're surrounded by spirits, living in a world infilled with soul, and that everything that exists is alive in some way. This applies not just to our own planet but to the whole universe, and not just to the material world but to all the many worlds people have talked about over the eons: the Underworld, the Nine Worlds of the Norse, the realm of Faerie. In the animist worldview, it's all very real and very much alive – and sentient or conscious in its own way, even if we can't understand it.

Some people like to equate animism with certain facets of quantum physics, such as quantum entanglement, to make it seem more scientific and less "primitive" (the idea that it is primitive stems from the now-discredited field of social

Darwinism that says that cultures of long ago must by definition be less evolved than the cultures of today). The physicist Nick Herbert has popularized the idea of quantum animism, in which consciousness permeates all matter and is an intrinsic part of it. He distinguishes his idea from the common, popular understanding of animism as a duality: that the world is made up of matter and spirit, which are two separate things. The problem with this distinction, this apparent duality, is that many of the traditional cultures that hold animism as their worldview don't really make such a clear division between the body and the spirit that inhabits it; to them, the two meld and blend in ways that can't be easily defined or separated. The body versus spirit issue appears to be a fairly modern one, possibly influenced by the Abrahamic religions (Judaism, Christianity, and Islam) with their insistence on the baseness of matter in contrast with the purity or "lightness" of the soul. Different cultures and traditions have their own understanding of the relationship between the material world and the spirit world, and modern shamans also have a wide range of points of view on this subject. Regardless, the distinction ends up being far less important than the idea that there is spirit within all things.

Ultimately, in animism we end up with the idea that it's not so much that everything has a spirit, but that everything is a spirit, and some spirits have physical forms while others don't. Or at least, they don't have physical forms in our world, though they may have them in the Underworld or some other realm. And if everything is spirit-filled, then animism permeates our everyday life, giving it a dimension beyond the mundane, mechanical explanation of how things work. Everything is connected; everything is alive; everything is, in its own way, conscious or sentient.

Why does it matter that we live in a spirit-filled world? Because just like us, those spirits have thoughts, desires, and intentions. They want and need things. And, because we're also spirits, they can interact with us, sometimes in ways we can't predict or control. We're not alone, and that's not a bad thing. It means we don't have to do things alone, without help. We have a soul connection, literally, with the rest of the world.

That's where shamanism comes in. A shaman is a specialist whose job is to have a relationship with the non-human spirits on behalf of their community. Even in cultures whose basic worldview includes animism, not everyone is capable of sensing those spirits or interacting with them. Some people have a natural talent for this kind of activity, but even they must be trained one way or another in order to protect themselves (the spirits aren't always friendly or kind) and so they can journey to find the spirits who can help the members of their community.

Through training by other human beings as well as directly by the spirits themselves, the shaman develops relationships with spirits who are helpful and supportive. These may be ancestors, animal spirit guides, spirits attached to the entire clan or community (such as totems), or simply individual spirits who are willing to assist the shaman. It's through these spirit helpers that the shaman is able to communicate safely and effectively with the rest of the spirit world. They are the "buffer zone" and sometimes the interpreter between the shaman and the spirits the shaman must interact with in order to bring healing, prosperity, and other assistance to their community.

There are many different methods of approaching shamanic work and actually performing the duties of the shaman. This part of shamanism – the "tech," if you will – varies from tradition to tradition and culture to culture. The various traditions have their own symbology, their own customary clothing for the shaman, their preferred methods for inducing trance (drums, rattles, incense, entheogens, dancing, singing, and more). But there is one universal, based in the worldview of animism: The shaman journeys, with the aid of spirit helpers, to interact with other spirits. The purpose of these journeys is to assist the shaman's community in one way or another.

A shamanic journey is sometimes called a soul flight. This means that the shaman's soul or spirit (or at least, part of it) travels away from their body. It can travel great distances on Earth and throughout space but it can also travel into other realms such as the Underworld. The various places the shaman visits are usually described in the mythos of their culture or tradition so they know what to expect when they reach their destination. In the animistic, shamanic worldview, all these realms are as real as the solid ground we walk on every day.

Many people who aren't shamans can interact with spirits to a certain extent during ordinary waking consciousness. For instance, some people will leave offerings outdoors for nature spirits and can sense the acceptance of those offerings, or occasionally the rejection of them. But the kind of contact and communication that's necessary for the work shamans do requires a much deeper level of interaction. They must deal with spirits who may be difficult to reach or who may not be friendly to humans. This requires journeying beyond ordinary consciousness and the everyday world.

What can all these spirits help a shaman do? In ancient times, a clan's shaman might journey to the spirit of an animal, deer for instance, for help in finding where the best herds were for hunting. After all, the people's very survival depended on finding enough to eat in the days before supermarkets. But for most people in the modern world, locating food is a simpler task these days. That doesn't mean there's nothing for a shaman to do anymore, though.

Health and well-being are important subjects for modern people, just like they were for our ancestors. A shaman can ask the spirits for help with physical illness and injury as well as mental health. The shaman can journey to find soul fragments that a person has lost due to trauma; this task often requires the assistance of spirit beings in order to locate the fragment and return it to its "owner." Shamans can also remove damaging energy and entities (spirits) that have latched onto people at various times in their lives. Shamans have undertaken these activities for generations on behalf of their communities.

Shamans also connect with the spirits of the land. In the distant past, they may have sought out the best places for their people to settle or to spend a season in. In the animist worldview, the land itself is a living thing, worthy of our respect and deserving of proper communication (via a shaman) if we're going to live off its resources. Even today, this is important: The shaman can help connect the people with the land where they live, with the mountain and river spirits and the spirits of the forests and meadows. Even cities and towns have land spirits; it's good to connect with the spirits wherever you live. This way, everyone can thrive because they all live with respect for one another.

In many parts of the world, there is also the issue of land being taken away from the indigenous people (who likely have an animist cosmology) and "developed" by invading groups. In these cases, the shaman can help heal some of the wounds made both to the land itself and to the ancestral native people whose culture and homes were destroyed. You've probably heard the joke about bad luck coming from having your house built over an Indian burial ground. That's only partly a joke, and it doesn't have to be a burial ground, just a beloved homeland. In the animist view, the people who lived there and had a deep connection with the land may have chosen to remain even after they died since they were tied on a spirit level with their home area. It's the shaman's job to communicate with these spirits and show them the respect they deserve, and perhaps help them move on to the afterlife.

Speaking of moving on to the afterlife, helping the spirit of the deceased journey from the realm of the living to the realm of the dead is one of the shaman's responsibilities. In this case the shaman acts as a psychopomp or deathwalker, helping the person's spirit find its way once the body releases it. In many traditions, the shaman sits with the dying person and helps their spirit pass over when the time comes. This kind of spirit release can also be done some time after the person's death, if the family feels they haven't crossed over yet. A shaman can also help to release "stuck" spirits of the dead at places like battlefields and sites of natural disasters.

Of course, all this shamanic activity relies on the underlying belief in the reality of the spirits the shaman is interacting with. These include the shaman's own helpers, guardians, and guides, which may appear to the shaman as humans, animals, mythical creatures, and a variety of other forms. The shaman also interacts with the spirits of the people they help, whether they're alive or not, for healing and deathwalking (which, in a sense, is a kind of healing). And the shaman interacts with other spirits in order to ask their aid for tasks the shaman can't complete alone.

There's another kind of spirit the shaman interacts with, one that isn't as obvious to those of us raised in the modern, secular world: the spirits of sacred objects. I mentioned above the idea of imbuing a created item with a spirit so that it becomes, in a sense, a living thing. This is exactly what happens when a shaman creates the special tools that are used in the various rituals of shamanic practice.

Not only do many shamans make their own drums and rattles, but they also perform special ceremonies in which they call a spirit into those sacred tools. Once a shaman's drum or rattle is inspirited, it becomes a living thing with which the shaman can interact. It becomes a helper just as much as the animal guides and the other helper spirits. In some traditions, shamans refer to their drum or rattle as the "horse" they "ride" into the other realms during an ecstatic journey. It's because of the living spirit of the instrument that it's able to help the shaman this way and provide the energy, momentum, and drive for far-reaching travels among the realms. It's certainly possible to journey using a non-inspirited drum or rattle, or even a recording of drumming and rattling. But having a living instrument brings a special sense of power to the work, another spirit helper for the labor of the journey and the sacred responsibility the shaman shoulders with every trance they undertake.

Some traditions include entheogens or other herbs as part of the technique for inducing ecstatic trance. In these situations, it's not just the chemicals within the plant that aid the shaman; the plant spirit is also an ally, leading the shaman to other worlds and sometimes even teaching them along the way. Many shamans receive help from a variety of plant spirits, not just the entheogens but healing herbs and even local trees and plants, if they're connecting with the land spirits of the area.

To the shaman, the whole world is alive and spirit-filled. The animistic worldview underlies shamanism and gives it not only meaning and purpose but also the mechanism by which shamanic practice works. It's the shaman's relationship with helper spirits – guides, guardians, plant spirit allies, inspirited tools – that allows them to journey to other realms and seek aid, knowledge, and healing for their communities. For the shaman, everything is connected; everything is relationship; everything is alive.

Beyond Cultural Appropriation and a Search for Authenticity – Reconnecting Shamanism with the Spirits of the Land

Jez Hughes

The last fifty years or so have seen a renaissance of shamanic practices across the West. This is a remarkable phenomenon given that most of our traditions were virtually wiped out. Firstly by organized religion and then the rational, scientific cosmological vision that followed. However, as the sixties saw the rise of a counter culture that embraced many seemingly discarded and archaic perspectives on reality, so a more widespread interest in indigenous spirituality and healing technologies began to emerge. This cultural-revolution laid the seeds of modern, Western shamanism which is today, once again, burgeoning in popularity.

Due to the perilous and uncertain present and future we face, politically, environmentally and spiritually, it is perhaps understandable that we have begun to look backwards to a seemingly more harmonious past, to reassess where we are heading as a culture.

This process hasn't been without problems though. A lot of the early shamanic pioneers in the West, the first teachers and authors, came from the US, especially the West Coast. This is understandable given that the States, although a Western nation, still had a living tradition on its soils, that of the indigenous North Americans. This land, still imbued with an indigenous tradition and spirit, has had an extraordinary influence on what we understand as modern Western cultural identity.

Such is the influence of Native American culture on shamanism, that many people associate shamanism primarily with Native American spirituality, even though the word is actually derived European/Asian, from the Tungus region of Siberia. It is important to remember, though, that this is a people who had a whole continent stolen from them, and who still exist predominantly in abject poverty on parcels of land called Reservations. The idea, then, of aspects of their cultural identity and spirituality being packaged up by the white man and called "shamanism", then often commercialized, understandably has created a lot of controversy and bad feeling. "Firstly, you stole our land, now you steal our culture" has been the, at times, legitimate complaint of indigenous northern Americans.

This issue of cultural appropriation, isn't unique to North American cultures. I work very closely with a tribe from central Mexico called the Wixarika, in Spanish known as the Huichol. Up until about six years ago, the Wixarika, were very closed off to the modern world and still, today, you have to be formally invited to visit their communities. They are very protective of their culture, which is largely how they've managed to hold on to it for tens of thousands of years.

When I visited them recently an elder spoke to us explaining how in the late sixties and early seventies people were becoming interested in their culture for the first time and requesting to visit. So they decided to open up a little and many anthropologist and spiritual seekers from the West came to stay. As the elder explained, these Westerners went on to make a lot of promises of how they would help the communities who, still today, live a very poor, subsistence based life farming some of the most difficult lands in Mexico. Like most indigenous peoples across the world, they also face regular persecution from the dominant society, so the appeal of having some Western help was obvious.

However, the Wixarika soon realized that their visitors, many of them anthropologists who made their careers from their field work with the Wixarika, soon forgot about them when they returned to their native countries and didn't keep the promises to help. Feeling very let down, the tribe decided to close down again, until very recently. He told this story without bitterness or recrimination but merely went on to say, "we'll just see how it goes this time round."

The mining of indigenous cultures for their spirituality, healing technologies and ceremonies, without giving back or even often acknowledging the source of what has been taken, is a big and often debated problem in modern shamanism.

This story of cultural appropriation usually begins with an indigenous culture realizing there are big problems facing the Earth and more particularly humanity. Often, like with the Wixarika, this is personal as one of the catalysts for the re-opening of their culture was the granting of oil concessions to a Canadian mining company in their most sacred lands. The spirits at the same time, told the Marakames (Shamans) that it is the white man who needs to be brought back in alignment with Mother Earth in order for humanity to survive and that they must share their traditions to facilitate this. Without this sharing of traditions, shamanism wouldn't be alive today in the West and we are incredibly indebted to the generosity of the indigenous people across the world who have done so.

The problems come, however, when this generosity is then used and abused by people who take these ways, adopt them as their own, and then package and sell them to others, often without having made the sacrifices necessary to do the required training. This creates a watering down of traditions that get buried under the commercial pressures that are the blight of modern, Western civilization. What begins then as healing becomes the opposite.

So what can be done to avoid this? In my experience of working with many different indigenous people and traditions, when they share their ways of connecting with the sacred it is done not so that we can go away and adopt them but rather as an inspiration to reconnect us to that which we have lost. A way of being in harmony with the world through the exquisite ceremonies and practices whose roots usually stretch far back in time.

Behind this is the simple shamanic truth, that there is an invisible world existing behind the manifest which has a profound influence on this one. And an interaction with that reality and the spirits that fill it, is not only possible, but beneficial to human life here. Also, perhaps most importantly, for that interaction to succeed there is a great deal of responsibility to "pay back" the beings of the invisible world. This responsibility, coming in the form of offerings, ceremonies, sacrifices etc., usually rests on the shoulders of the shaman, who is the intermediary between the invisible worlds of spirits and humans.

There is a very profound teaching in this, one that we have lost in the modern world and which is at the heart of indigenous spirituality and shamanism: the whole of nature and its successful functioning is based on reciprocity. This is the role of the shaman, to ensure that the human side of that reciprocity is met. In return, they are granted powers, through their connection with the spirits, which mean they are able to serve their community by healing and problem solving on behalf of others.

A while back I asked my students where does the power to heal that the shaman uses come from? They all said, the spirits which of course is correct. However, it is only half the answer. What is often overlooked in modern shamanism is that the real power the shaman utilizes comes from the land. The spirits don't just exist in some abstract Otherworld that we just travel to in trance, as is often taught in modern shamanism when it is stripped of its cultural trappings. The spirits are representatives of the land and the natural environmental powers that keep the world functioning and in balance.

Hence a shaman might draw their power from the spirit of a local river, or mountain, or other sacred place. There might be an animal that is the guardian spirit or representative of that sacred place and the shaman works with the spirit of the animal as well. The shaman might work with spirits of the sky gods and goddesses, but it will always be the sky above them, not an imaginary sky. Or they might work directly with the sun or the rain, again though there will be intermediaries often in the form of animal spirits which the shaman communicates with in order to interpret the message coming from these larger forces.

The animal spirits will be local to the tribe and community, as what exists in the Otherworld is always a reflection of here. They won't be those they've read about in a book or seen pictures of as a child. Because indigenous spirituality is always closely linked with the practical, the animals that provide the most in the physical reality, for example, the Buffalo in North American plains tribes who provided food, shelter and clothes will be the most sacred and honored as such. In tribes in Europe it might be tree spirits such as the Oak, who helped the people so much in the physical reality that held this status of most revered.

In short, shamanism, wherever it is practiced and in whichever way, is always anchored to the local environment. This crucial grounding of traditions in time and space, which gives the traditions their context and also their unique colors and flavors, is something that is often missing in the way modern shamanism is approached and taught in the West.

The main reason for this is that shamanism as a concept was invented by academics, so its history is one of being born from the halls of the intellect. One of the advantages of the intellect is its ability to collate diverse ideas into singular concepts, as it did with shamanism. One of the disadvantages though, is it can be detached from the here and now and physical reality, which is also, I believe, what has happened with the concept of shamanism.

What this leads to in a practical sense is the top down imposition of traditions on landscapes that may not suit them. We had this a lot with organized religion, when something like Christianity that was born in the desert and had that emphasis on sky worship alongside dry, ascetic principals was imposed on the green and watery lands of much of Europe. This meant that the land and tree spirits which were predominantly honored and worshipped previously were replaced with abstract figures from a story that came from a land far away.

In the modern day this still happens, when some Native traditions are swallowed whole and their cosmology is imposed on an environment that doesn't best suit them. It is the same level of incongruence if it's a tradition from the Lakota or Christianity. Yes, there has always been cross-fertilization of traditions and that still happens, but for shamanism to land fully in the West and grow some strong roots, I believe the primary focus has to be listening to the regional land spirits again.

Because, in the end, all traditions arose originally out of human society's interaction with their environments. The shaman's role, as explored earlier, is through communication with the spirits of the environment to ensure the smooth running of that relationship.

Localizing traditions again might also help solve one of the perennial debates in modern shamanism of whether a Westerner can call them self a shaman having not been born or initiated in a tribal culture that has a living tradition. Basically this often comes down to a Western obsession with authenticity. Many different spiritual paths suffer from this in the modern age which often comes across as a kind of underlying competitiveness among people to constantly prove their authenticity – by how many different teachers and cultures they have learnt from, what equipment they have, what songs have been learnt, how many ceremonies taken part in, how many different plant teachers worked with, how pure a practice is, whether someone calls themselves a shaman or not etc., etc.

My sense is that beneath this need to prove authenticity is a gaping hole of spiritual confidence that comes from being born in a culture where shamanic traditions have been lost. That hole cannot be filled by merely transplanting other traditions that aren't indigenous to the area. It can, however, start to be healed by the reconnection of ourselves with the local land spirits that surround us. When we connect to these all the questions of authenticity naturally fall away, because it is nature that holds the key to authenticity, which no amount of learning about different traditions can match. They are the bosses here after all, that is the bedrock of shamanism; it is the spirits who decide and it is them who are ultimately the teachers.

Connecting with the spirits that are local to wherever you are also guards against cultural appropriation as, naturally, when we listen well enough, ways of practice and traditions will be taught by the land spirits and their representatives. These may have been inspired by work with indigenous cultures, as they are so far ahead of us in terms of shamanic practice, however, it will also be heavily influenced by the spirit of place we are working with.

The first step of this process comes from active engagement with the local spirits, and the medium for that is offerings. This is the way the shaman begins the communicative channels, honoring the sacred rule of reciprocity by giving first. Then, through utilizing the various methods of going into trance, the shamans allow themselves to be open enough to receive the wisdom, guidance and gifts of power that come from the environmental powers they are connecting with. Thus restoring balance to the human and invisible worlds, and being major catalysts for the healing of the Earth and the human guests upon Her.

Another aspect of this is the honoring of our own ancestors and, if they aren't originally from the land where we now reside, introducing them to the ancestors who are from there and are now buried in the ground. This connecting of ancestral lineages can then start to heal some of the wounds the huge displacement of peoples has had on the modern world. It also will help again with issues of authenticity as we all have ancestors, going back far enough, who practiced these ways. Though, in order to get through to our most ancient ancestors we may need to undertake some ancestral healing on the most recent members of our bloodline residing in the Otherworld, as they are the first step to us reconnecting to the power and gifts of our ancestral lineage.

Shamanism ultimately is about healing. Healing and rebalancing the invisible forces that hold this world together, be they bloodline ancestors or the older ancestors of the land and cosmos that gave birth to our home here. Through this emphasis on healing, shoots of growth can then emerge. Traditions that have been lying dormant in the earth and, in particular, the sacred sites our ancestors worshipped, will be re-membered as shamans begin to listen to songs of the land and piece back together old ways of being in harmony with it.

Through this process shamanism has the opportunity to land fully in the West and become a living breathing tradition once more, something that can be of great assistance to us as we move forward through these times of great change and upheaval.

Modern Shamanism, the Middle World, and Ego

S. Kelley Harrell

The breezes at dawn have secrets to tell you
Don't go back to sleep!
You must ask for what you really want.
Don't go back to sleep!
People are going back and forth
across the doorsill where the two worlds touch,
The door is round and open
Don't go back to sleep!
— Jalaluddin Rumi

Soul travel into the Middle World is a deeply shrouded topic in modern shamanism. In the more prevalent contemporary schools of shamanism, Middle World work is at worst not taught, and at least glossed over, which may be more detrimental. The Mid-strata is the place of directly engaging the environment – the land, weather, elements, animals, plants, trees. Skipping the spiritual realm to which we are most directly connected, the one that birthed our cells and fused our soul to form has created a lack of understanding of how our spiritual sense of self is directly related to the Middle World. As a result, the modern shamanism movement hasn't matured fully into the depth of work the planet needs.

I confess, I don't resonate with the triple world model we've all been given in the modern shamanism context: Upper, Lower, and Middle World. From the beginning of my formal study, wider nuances of strata met me beyond the dreaming, and they never functioned as the box described. Rather, I experience a diverse model likened to the Nine Worlds of the Old Norse path, with Midgardr as the predominant human realm.

Triplicity is, however, the common cosmology, and I address it as such for discussion. Many traditional cultures present a triad perspective of cosmology, which is perhaps why it came into such strong use on the contemporary path. We had to start somewhere. The ancient appeal of the triple model is that prior to modern psychology, it gave narrative to the levels of our awareness: conscious, preconscious, and unconscious. Still relevant, this threesome comprises our cosmological humanness: Transpersonal (collective soul), Ego/Body, and Soul.

In terms of agreeing on a common framework, the triple world construct is a simple base cosmology presented to beginner shamans. When we all start with the same structure, it makes the details easier to teach, cope with, and support. Having a common grasp of cosmology while learning shamanism provides the necessary rungs of the ladder to give the brain a methodology for changing wave states; a process which is required to shift from beta, or our waking awareness mode, into theta state, the wave of cognizant dreaming.

As well, working from such a common model allows the events that take place in the spirit world to have meaning for the shaman. Meaning usually comes in the form of beings who act as guides or spirit allies in our earthly endeavors. These sacred kin and their symbolism may hail from cherished mythologies, religious paths, sacred lands, or some other personal significance that connects directly to the chosen world model.

Having a firm understanding of cosmology as the means to access other realms triggers the brain's innate mechanisms to remember the events. It gives us a pneumonic bookmark, which allows us to hold the extraordinary spot we encountered in dreamtime, while we interpret and apply it in the mundane. Quite simply, it provides gentle, informed transition in and out of trance, and a framework through which to carry out sacred missions in the everyday.

That said, it's possible to implement more complex or simplistic soul realm models. The number of worlds isn't significant as long as the observed cosmology has meaning for the shaman. To that end, I encourage my students and Initiates to explore beyond the triple world model.

In some way, every structure of cosmology comprises some unseen layer of the immediate mundane. Such is the strata commonly referred to as the Middle World. To hold it in context of the triple worldview, exploring each realm therein, imparts a deeper understanding of how each works.

The Lower World, sometimes referred to as the Underworld, is the typical starting point of spiritual exploration for beginners. It's been quite demonized as "Hell," though in the shamanic context, it carries no connotation of punishment or wrongdoing. I consider it the deeper well of Earth's magick, though it's presented as a wild, yet pristine land of Nature-based guides (animals, birds, plants, trees, etc.), possibly totems, who hold timeless wisdom about Earth's being-ness, and advice regarding how to engage Nature for healing in the mundane. This layer is the unconscious aspect, the soul, which is deeply rooted in how we experience raw Nature. Often healing of soul, emotion, memories, and ancestors is done here.

Likewise, the Upper World is erroneously associated with "Heaven," though it's in no way a place of reward or good deeds. It is often experienced as celestial, a bright cloud-filled sky, though for some it spans a dark, void-like expanse, or a fantasy land. It's the place of Spirit Guides, saints, ascended masters, teachers, and higher aspects of Self. This realm is transpersonal space, containing angelic humanoids and deities. Healing done here usually involves the mind, collective soul experiences, and intellectual matters.

The Middle World is loosely considered the spiritual expression of the Earth. I think of it as the point that we can directly engage Earth's astral self, our planet's unseen, its soul.

The Middle World is the destination most closely related to our waking reality, in which suffering spirits linger, Nature Spirits dwell, dreams occur, the strata of beings we know as faeries, elves, and sylphs, etc. reside, and it provides a good place for observation of the Divine in our mundane lives. This layer is related to matters of ego, body, and our personal development.

Where the Lower and Upper Worlds are valued as quasi-personal spaces, the Middle World is space shared by all souls engaging in the earthly realm. All space is ultimately shared, though the distinction in how we use the worlds in shamanic care plays a vital role in our attitude toward and work done in the Middle World. As we are most closely tied to the Middle World, this space is presented with all the personal biases and filters (or lack thereof) that influence how we perceive it. Because we physically exist in the Middle World as spirits in form, we are emotionally involved with it, and the experiences we have there often challenge our belief systems. As a result, in this realm it's hard to release expectations of what we think it should be compared to how we experience it in form, what we have been told it is, and what benefit we should receive by engaging it.

Among such challenges is programming that urges us to fit certain spiritual experiences into dualities of "good" or "evil," "positive" or "negative." As shamanic worldview doesn't inherently carry such compartmentalization, visits in the Middle World, in particular, can trigger crisis when they don't mesh with our beliefs or personal truths. As shamans whose job is to deconstruct an accepted broken reality and reconstruct it to support a new functional reality, such judgments serve no purpose in our work. Still, so little emphasis is put on the Middle World in modern shamanism, it would seem that leaving it out is such a judgment.

Traditional shamanists recognize the Middle World immediately upon selection as shaman. In fact, the ability to function healthily in the spiritual layer of earthly being is required before progressing to other realms. Only in the modern context are we warned off the Middle strata as if it's a cowboy frontier, a lawless terrain poised to strip us of our safety, sanity, and personhood. How can we hope to successfully explore, let alone establish reciprocal relationship with other spiritual realms if we don't know how to function within the one we were created? Indeed, it is the most challenging realm of soul work, which is no reason that it should be skipped. In fact, we can't skip it. We're born into it as animists.

Animism at its simplest is the observation that all things have a soul, and through that connection, can intercommunicate. The Middle World is the seat of animism, of which shamanism is one expression. As children we arrive with the innate gift of enlivening everything we contact – toy animals, food, trees, invisible friends. In that interaction is our first recognized experience of being a soul, and the awareness of such in others. Animism brings our first recognition of tribe, of our first awareness of *chosen* community. However, as we age and are confronted with the limitations of the five senses, the challenges of the formed experience, we exchange animism for measurable teachings grounded in surviving and thriving. We aren't taught that we can hold both.

In that light, modern shamanism has taken a similar tack. Michael Harner is credited with bringing shamanism to the West, and largely his structure of Core Shamanism set the precedent for minimizing Middle World involvement. To make shamanism safe, personable, and legal, shortcuts were taken to make it accessible to Western culture. The Middle World was one of them. As a result, its significance as a spirit realm through which we live and breathe isn't tied into animistic living. The inability to see it as both the place where we dwell *and* as inherently holy has contributed to the idea that sacred space is isolated and rare. That cultural tenet coupled with the spiritual rejection of it in modern shamanism was a tragic omission that has rippled out a long-lasting impact for the planet.

Foremost is the loss of our direct relationship to Nature, personally and collectively. Few of us know how to survive in the wild. We no longer know how to thrive with the land. Not enough of us can read its omens. At a spiritual level, this means the land no longer recognizes us as community; rather, it sees us as a stranger, if not a threat. Directly because of our actions and avoidance, Land Elders that have stood vigil for thousands of years have parted, taking with them wisdom and teachings vital to human development. The Fae, Giants, and other kin no longer trust us because we haven't actively, consistently stood with them. Many of us don't even know how to.

Our destruction of natural resources, radically increased population, accelerated impact on climate change, and reluctance to embrace sustainable and green technologies has taken a direct toll on our spiritual relationship with the Middle World. The lack of that healthy relationship has likewise impacted our personal and spiritual development.

Consider that the Middle World is solely focused on work that challenges ego and body, and that the ego's job is to protect the body. When we think of the Middle World in those terms and how little attention it gets, many things come sharply into focus. First, by forsaking Nature as a primal influence on our spiritual natures, we have also failed to develop our egos – which the New Age has taught aren't spiritual components. Ego is viewed as shadow, which many schools of thought believe and teach is "bad," and cannot be changed. Conversely, through ecopsychology, we learn that the development of early humankind's ego was based on our relationship with Nature. We observed and imitated animal and plant kingdoms to achieve harmony in group dynamics, interpersonal relationships, and to learn to live in relationship with Nature itself. In Nature, we learned to master conflict, within and without. The result of this co-development with Nature was a matured ego.

Second, by not delving into ego, we have left the body vulnerable. Ecopsychology teaches that the body and Nature are connected, if not combined. Sickness in one is reflected in the other. By not developing our egos we have never collectively matured to that very realization. Without the discernment of the ego, we find fear and an inability to draw on reason and logic to make personal choices, the collective result of which is a society of distrust and disconnection. Nature becomes excluded. We lash out at each other.

Third, in leaving the body vulnerable, we have avoided our role in Nature, which is to realize we are wholly part of it and must live in accordance with its rules. Without understanding our place in Nature, we can neither protect it nor prosper within it. Instead, we have become sick, which has created a sickness that wraps the planet. We haven't just created the crisis, we *are* it.

Our lack of focus on ego in modern shamanism has created a movement largely based on and stalled by self-healing. Given the lack of animistic worldview in the West and no widely cast shamanistic tradition, we arrive at shamanism wounded, in need. There's no fault or blame in this fact of our cultural awakening. However, when we cease to move beyond self-healing, when we opt not to delve into those darker, shadow parts of the Middle Self, we're essentially avoiding the greater work needed in the Middle World. We're refusing to embrace the vital components of the completed initiation into shamanhood and vital sense of duty to community, both of which are the fully realized role of shaman. Both require mastery of the ego, which means mastery of the Middle World.

By embracing these components the Middle World becomes not just our most immediate experience of the spiritual, it becomes the layer in which we are *most* directly connected and interconnected. Through that weaving we shape and are shaped by our initiations in form. Our success with those initiations determines our ability as shamans, which is most directly demonstrated in the Middle World. In that light, it's not just our classroom and foremost experience and expression of community, it's the seat of our duty, of our calling.

The success of the planet relies on our success navigating and mastering the Middle World. It requires that we find ourselves in Nature, and vice versa, and in doing so become active animists. This primal truth is what has allowed traditional shamanism to sustain and thrive for thousands of years.

The pattern of using shamanism as a self-healing tool has left us only engaging the spirit realm when we need something. Our privilege has taught us that our need is enough to warrant our salvation, that saviors abound, and saviors never need saving. Nonetheless, Nature has been presenting need for a long time, and as a result we're all in crisis. Not having responded to Nature's need all these years has damaged that bond, and left us incapable of saving ourselves. However, the more we tend Nature, the stronger the bond between us, so that day-to-day circumstance improves for both, and when we have an emergency, the bridge is already in place for assistance to be given. The trust and the strength are reciprocally solid for reaching between worlds.

This is the work that isn't taught. In fact, it can't be taught in a weekend workshop or extended course. It only comes of the long-meted, mentored saturation of a person on the path, tending, living, and breathing it through, every day.

Don't ask Nature to teach this. Don't expect it to. In our culture is the pattern of demanding the victim teach the oppressor not to victimize. Instead, learn by doing better. Remember that as big a concept as Nature is – planet and beyond – it's right under our feet. It's our backyard, and sprigs tufting the cracks of sidewalks. It's the creatures of our immediate bioregions, the spirits of the land we live on. Care for them. Engage them, without expectation.

Now isn't the time of heroic strides and solitary efforts. Honoring the Middle World takes more than one of us, or even a few. It takes a collaborative community effort of each of us working where we stand to engage the Nature where we live, not just once or on sacred occasions, but tending it ongoing, so that when we reach into the Middle World, it *can* reach back. In this way, we look after it and each other. Our responsibility to All Things is to be present in that relationship *all the time*, not just when it's convenient. *Only tending over time creates this relationship.*

Our success depends on bonding with others who understand the work before us all. It's the time of humility and tending, the long slog of doing right by Nature, solely because it hasn't been done in a very long time, because it likely won't become the sanctioned way for a very long time – if ever. It's the time of delving into our own shadows, and realizing that the Middle World is our best teacher to accomplish that healing, well. The express purpose of this realm is to force us to release our deepest wounds, and through the initiation of doing so, to understand impeccably what our duty to community is, to Nature – thus, ourselves.

And this initiation will not save us, not as we currently exist. No effort we make now will reverse what has been done, though it will redeem some part of what we did, who we are, who we are becoming, and the ancestral burden we have carried.

Hear the call of the Middle World, and in doing so allow the primal within. Rise to it. Bring offerings, every day, in the form of water, blessings, gratitude, volunteering – whatever is most doable – to Nature. Whatever this tending dredges from within, meet it head-on and open-armed. Find the teachers who can instruct in how to breathe it through. Court the healers who can not only heal the soul but join in, to share the work of shifting our ultimate vantage point from one that is egocentric to one that is cosmocentric.

Shamanism is a path of balance. Our success in achieving it lies in the Middle World.

Shamanism for Inner Soul Work

Julie Dollman

There is a misnomer around spirituality and practice. It concerns the idea that anyone who considers themselves as "spiritual" is either a bit weird or quite strange, often classed as being "one of those."

Confusion often arises in statements regarding whose practice is better than somebody else's. For most generic spiritual practitioners, the inner core of what spirituality entails becomes lost in translation. After all, there is a clear difference between the term Religion and Spirituality. It is better understood that religion is an external practice, wherein the follower gears their practice to a set of rules and edicts that belong to a formalized code of repetition as directed by the Clergy, Priest or by studying a Bible or another holy book. Therefore Religion is far more succinctly concerned with form, ritual, and hierarchy.

Wherein, spirituality explains the process of "inner soul work," it encompasses a set of esoteric practices that focus more on the internal landscape, one which becomes an intimate and personal journey into the mysteries that are only found beneath the skin of the tradition we wish to follow.

To sum up these differences in an easily understandable manner, Religion focuses on a premise of how to form your spiritual practice and the inner soul work of spirituality; the focus is more on one's integrity and purpose. The world today has veered away from an authentic existence and has replaced it by stepping into a realm of materialism.

Many who live in the world today find the more we have, regarding material possessions, and the more money we earn and spend, substantiates an illusion that informs us that this is all that matters. This idea creates a gulf, and we become less connected to anything that is inside us, let alone to an omnipresent being or creator. Herein lies an inherent modern-day phenomenon. To decide which came first and what the cause was of this phenomenon is to understand better the need for us to do "inner soul work."

From the beginning of the patriarchal usurpation of religion and its practices, stolen and revamped from the Priestesses, the feminine principle and old-religions retreated to the underground, where s/he could practice and remain in service to the Matrilineal ancient religions until it became endemically unsafe and dangerous to do so. As power, laws and wars became the norm for society, Kings and the Hierarchical system of Priesthoods of the masculine became more focused on stealing land, gaining power, and accumulating the spoils of material possession gained during these raids and battles. The Priesthoods' focus was to ensure everyone served their religious notions, those that went against the law of the land received horrendous punishment, often resulting in death. As the world and man evolved and became more modern, religions that were once the forefront of society began to lose their grip on the population. Why?

Holes began to appear as humanity and its flaws became transparent. Tales of violence and injustice rose to the surface, including, sexual abuse, cruelty and dark behaviors. In the late 1960s, we began to see the cracks emerge as free, independent self-expression began to develop in the younger generation. As they became suspicious of these so-called holders of divinity they witnessed religion begin its decline by falling out of fashion and favor; attributed to a lack of attachment to religious form and, then, further dismay due to the "flaws of man."

A vast elopement away from religious hierarchy left a void, a huge gaping hole, one we desperately began to fill with alcohol, drugs, sex, gambling and hedonistic behaviors, coupled with a deeper need to gain material possession. After 20 years or so, around two percent of the population of the globe began to seek a new way to fill this void. Leaving organized religions, people became curious and began to explore alternative modes of soul expression. Meditation, Yoga, Buddhism, Angel Therapy, Reiki, naming a few of the paths that were sought out. Then suddenly, shamanism in its myriad of forms became popular. As people began to identify more with Native American guides, Celtic Shamanism, South American Shamanism and Norseman anthologies, more and more avenues began to open. Hundreds of books have been written to guide those seeking more, as well as millions of classes offered.

Within a short space of ten years, Shamanism has become the "new in-thing!" However, problems soon rose to the surface, as people began to enjoy the rites and rituals, ceremonies and healing techniques. Many loved to dress-up in pagan attire, wearing feathers and shaking a rattle or banging a hand-made drum. Shamans love to traverse the other realities of the Underworld, the Middle world, and the Upper Realms, journeying to find answers and to talk to their power animal guides.

We love the escape and adventure of these non-reality realms, we all love the idea of escaping daily to the higher echelons of Divine interaction, it's the best experience anyone can have without the use of substances. While busy traversing, this too can become a distraction or an avoidance of dealing with the work we are here to do. The work involves "inner soul work," such as clearing karmic sludge accumulated over lifetimes and healing the ancestors through connecting and communicating with them regularly. We have, in all honesty, become an alternative tribe of escape artists; escaping the reality that has been carved out for us under the rule of a patriarchy – one dominated solely by their human law.

Shamanism offers us the chance to begin the journey of the "hero." The hero or heroine in this epic adventure is of course yourself – the "I" or the individual consciousness which made plans to return to the Earth dimension to continue its proposed soul lessons and increment this somewhat elusive pursuit of "enlightenment." The contract we make to do this is a continuum of required learning incorporating the care of the body and mind we inhabit by adopting a practice of releasing any energy which inhibits us, and of course, ensuring we walk this earth with humility, grace, and gratitude.

After we leave the Earth plane, as a result of our death, we return home to the next environment. We spend time in quiet reflection as we recapitulate our last life spent here on Earth. We review our escapades and our interactions, and we take account of our deeds. We collate the karmic load we took with us to ascertain if, and how, we "cleared the sludge." Finally, we review any additional karma collated along the way. After an unaccountable and inordinate amount of time spent expunging these karmic residues, it's time to reincarnate to Earth once more.

As we alight into the third dimension, down the ethereal silver cord, we adopt a new organic body. As we grow with our birth families, an already known lineage of ancestry, we are wiped clean of information containing previous incarnations. As we begin fresh and seemingly "new," we instigate a new voyage all over again. The events and experiences we encounter are often a heady mix of the good, the bad and the ugly. The obligatory life lessons are gathered and learned by the way we handle ourselves and cope. These lessons become the varying themes of a new life map as we carve a new script for ourselves. As we grow from child to man, we find we are immersed in the lives of others, somehow adopting and taking on board more and more energy, often unnecessary. There is a hidden requirement of learning how to "get on" and be in relationship with others. In adopting relationship roles, we often realize it is the relationship we have with ourselves, first and foremost, that is, habitually, the main importance of experiencing Earth.

During our life walk, a deep undercurrent of uneasiness

begins to rumble and pulsate within. In our attempt to make sense of these mysterious rumblings, from the point of human knowledge, it isn't strange or unusual to deem it purely as another of life's rocky paths to stumble along. There may be something deeper at play, a "proviso" of sorts that has been pre-set deep in our DNA and set to activate at the right time. To urge us to seek wholeness once more, and in doing so, we achieve wisdom personified in this current lifetime. It becomes the proverbial secret, an unknown set of requirements, hidden and kept undisclosed even from ourselves! Perhaps it is the elusive life purpose everyone is eager to know about, a further catalyst to urge us to undertake our inner soul work.

With Shamanism, there are many tools that will assist us in doing the "inner soul work." There are clues available to help understand what this work entails; there are themes comprising repeated patterns of incidents occurring throughout life, such as abandonment, loneliness, abuse, violence, disconnection, feelings of confusion, anxiety, fear and depression. Look at the recurrence of physical illnesses you are prone to, there are many clues available.

One of the biggest clues involves the ancestors and the lives they lived, the clues are there, held in the stories or myths. There are also clues held in a certain similarity concerning types of illnesses that befall a family; Cancers; Heart problems; Allergies; all these synchronicities add up to solve the puzzle. In the West it is common for us to almost forget about those who have passed. Even though we tend the graves there is little or no further contact with our ancestors past the markings on the tombstone. In other cultures around the world it is still a widespread practice to recognize and communicate with the dead. Not via mediums, but more in a personal, honoring way. The saying goes like this, "it is through our ancestors, we live now." If not for them, we wouldn't be here. To explore this even further, the cultures who still recognize, communicate, celebrate and revere their ancestral bloodline would warn us that to neglect the ancestors means we lack their protection, and without this we open the door to evil or dark spirits, creating negativity, chaos, strife, separation anxiety and mental illnesses in our lives.

In shamanic practice and teachings, whichever path you follow or feel inherently connected towards, the priority is to heal yourself. To undertake the journey of the wounded healer asks us to heal the wounds or traumas we have had in our lives by releasing and letting them go. This process should also include an offer of forgiveness to those who have caused harm to you. Bear in mind to offer forgiveness to yourself, especially if you, too, have caused harm in any way through harming others, self-sabotage or remorse. There is another saying that is relevant here, and it states, "It isn't the event that will be recalled, but everyone will remember how you reacted and dealt with the event." Be mindful that it is our actions that other people end up defining us by.

Shamanism requires us to take responsibility for our healing and personal practices. Ceremony and ritual are lacking in the majority of homes. We think we can solve problems in the realm of our mind-matrix, often, only to find it comes down to a choice or a battle or even worse, empathy. Modern-day teachings and family beliefs urge us to conform or to figure things out for ourselves. If only we would surrender ourselves to our higher guidance and trust that all will be as it should be then this alone would begin to alleviate pressure from our shoulders.

There is a misconception that lies in this fact; many people seek the services of mediums, tarot card and angel guidance readers. Many attend alternative healers; they lie on plinths while listening to soothing music, snuggled warmly under a soft blanket. They hold one thing dear to their hearts, and this is to receive guidance in the following areas, for example:

"Take all my pain and suffering away."

"Tell me what's going to happen in my future."

"Tell me what to do about my lover/husband/sister/friend, the one who causes me so much hurt and grief."

Underneath these desperate needs, is the desire for someone else to do the work for them by waving a magic wand, or by solving life's problems. The sad thing is, practitioners can only guide and begin the healing journey for their clients. Clients come to see me from all over the world. Before we begin the process of "healing," I explain to them that I am only part of a four-part equation of help they can get to attain completeness and healing as there are many facets and illusions of life. There are four aspects of importance that are required to be in complete harmony and balance to ensure wellness and clarity.

There is the realm of the Physical; this realm requires us to make better choices and to adopt a healthier approach to life so that we can maintain and care for this organic body we are borrowing, as we undertake our Earth journey. If we do not change the way we eat, or if we continue to choose processed foods, then further on, down the line, we could see a propensity to certain illnesses. If we do not go out and walk, swim, and exercise, then not only do we continue to become disconnected from nature, we also do not maintain our body to sustain its strength for the epic journey.

Then there is the next realm, the realm of the Psychological, the matrix of the mind. Here we are asked to be reticent in our thought processes, to be conscious of not allowing this realm to become dominant or to hijack our thought processes. It is the place of beliefs, not only those we hold true ourselves but also, the beliefs of our families and external institutions that become etched into a mind-matrix, which can either define or manipulate our freedom of thoughts and ideas. If this realm isn't attended to carefully, we could also allow fear in, which may derail us or push us towards depression or anxiety because we do not feel we have captaincy over ourselves.

The third realm is the realm of Emotions. Many of us know

this realm intimately, here we churn and process, we become overwhelmed and confused. Often, from here we drive our thought processes and ensuing actions. We lay ourselves bare in an onslaught of feelings and expressions, all in an attempt to be heard, seen or helped. When these emotions become all consuming, we are in danger of sinking, becoming lost in a dark sea, at risk of becoming engulfed and losing our precious essence.

Last and by no means least, there is the realm of Spirituality, the inner hard drive of our lineages and purpose for life. Some people spend 50-60 years trying to find their way back into the safe hands of our Creator. And yet many are in denial of following the maps offered to find the elusive "holy grail" by failing to listen to the sacred laws which are there to help and offer a lifeline. A lifeline that will, when it's time, show them the way home. Without spirituality, ceremony and ritual we become lost and confused. We fall into an entrapment of an illusion of materialism with a golden ticket to "the great void."

When you next visit a Shaman or other healer, understand that they can only help you clear and heal to a point. There is also a joint contract, one that asks you to bring into balance other aspects of your being – change nothing, then nothing changes. Each of these four realms and aspects must be attended to equally for optimum benefit. Healing and divinations can only partly clear the inner, unhealed aspects of ourselves. Therefore we must cleanse these by undertaking the journey of the hero or heroine and work on ourselves. Divinations, Oracles and Counsel can facilitate and offer incredible healing by putting together pieces of the puzzle. Only the work we undertake on ourselves can guarantee a peaceful mind, or wellness, or invoke joy into our lives. It is therefore, first and foremost, our responsibility to be courageous so we can face adversity and stand firm in the face of fear, taking all necessary help, guidance and actions to heal and change. This is the core of adopting and undertaking the work of the "inner soul."

Animals and Healing

Hearth Moon Rising

If you were helping a friend who was depressed, what animal would you turn to for advice? Can you name an animal who could help you channel a healing dance? How could animals help you enhance your shamanic practice and become a more effective healer?

Shamanism is, at its core, a way of healing through magic. Even if that healing is about becoming right with the world on a social, material, or emotional level, it's still about healing. While mental, emotional, and physical spheres of being interconnect, in this article I want to concentrate on the physical healing powers various animals can bring to shamanic interventions. I am going to restrict my focus to traditional magical belief originating in Europe and the Mediterranean, although I have gleaned additional information from my own observations of animals and from my own practice.

There is no "healing animal." All animals possess healing powers, often a great many powers. Sometimes the best animal to interact with in a healing setting is the one you have a strong connection with in the present or have successfully worked with in the past. The information about the following animals is meant to add to your fund of knowledge. This information can be integrated into spells or conscious dream work, the animal in question can be called upon to lead a shamanic journey focused on a solution to a physical ailment, or a picture or effigy of the animal can be placed in a workspace or bedroom to invoke the animal's healing power on a continual yet subconscious level.

In the past, animal healing power was usually obtained through ingesting that animal, with or without an accompanying spell. This was a form of magic, not nutrition, different from the sleepiness that occurs after a cup of hot milk or a large turkey dinner, which has a chemical basis. Most of these animals do not contain compounds with healing potential. The most notable exceptions to this are in the toad and frog families, where the skins of some species have antibacterial or psychoactive effects. Another exception would be forms of animal fat such as bear grease or lanolin, which have healing applications for the skin. Despite these and other exceptions, animal healing usually occurs on a subtle plane.

Dead animals or parts of dead animals have also been utilized in spells, most commonly during animal sacrifice. Today these practices arouse spirited ethical debate. Even the use of animal products such as leather, feathers, milk, or eggs can provoke disagreement. Fortunately it is possible to connect directly with an animal being (call it spirit, mother, deity, queen, familiar, or oversoul) to obtain a healing intervention.

Many of the animals I describe here are considered insignificant or repulsive. This is not coincidental. Often the most revered animal healers, such as the toad or the pig, were considered competing deities by monotheistic religious authorities, and so revulsion against these animals was consciously planted and consistently nurtured. Animals such as the owl or the wolf have been rehabilitated to a large extent in the past few hundred years because most Western cultures glorify violence and respect dominance, and these animals are seen – sometimes inaccurately – as reinforcing these values.

Some animals are overlooked as healers because they are dangerous, but not in a sexy way. The mouse falls into this category. Mice carry disease and destroy grain, so it is easy to revile them rather than understand them in a more complete way or enlist their help in combating the diseases they spread.

Here are some examples of the healing powers of animals.

The **bear** is associated with the goddess Artemis and healthy childbirth. The shrine of Artemis Brauron was dedicated to the health of mothers and children. As an omnivore, the bear knows about healing herbs and can instruct the healer in their use.

Bees are believed to harvest and concentrate the healing properties of flowers. Bee products are still used as a base for herbal ointments and herbs taken internally. Bee products have also been used in magic to enhance vision and hearing. Honey has antibacterial properties and keeps ointments from spoiling. Honey soothes sore throats and suppresses coughs. Honey was once considered an aphrodisiac and an essential part of weddings. Invoke the bee for infections and skin disorders as well as impotence and low sexual desire. Bees can also be summoned for lifting depression. This is related not only to the blissful intoxication of mead but to the contented buzz of a well-functioning hive. To attract bees for ritual, hum in a contented way yourself. It is worth noting that a considerable amount of bee healing folklore is directed toward keeping hives happy and productive. This includes speaking respectfully to bees, keeping hives informed of developments within their human family, waking up hives at the end of winter with knocks, cymbals, or ceremonies, and making offerings of cakes eaten at weddings and funerals. Among the many bee goddesses are Aphrodite, Cybele, Artemis of Ephesus, The Thraiae, Brigid, and Neith.

The **cat** goddess Bast was revered in Egypt as a nurturing mother; especially supplicated for healthy children and easy childbirth. Most books on ancient Egypt neglect to mention that early childhood mortality was astronomical in the Nile Valley even for aristocrats, much higher than in other city states in the Mediterranean. For this reason charms and spells for healthy children were an ongoing preoccupation. Feline allies are also appealed to for relief from fevers and insomnia.

Dogs have a long history of shamanic healing, probably going back to their domestication. Dogs were encouraged to lick sores and open wounds to both cure and prevent infections. Saliva from most mammals, even humans, has antibacterial properties, but there are probably fewer diseases that can be transferred from dogs to humans as opposed to between humans, and dogs are generous when it comes to bestowing their slobber. So powerful were doggy kisses believed to be that dogs were encouraged to lick patients with fevers even in the absence of skin eruptions. Understand that I am not saying that you should allow dogs to lick patients with wounds or compromised immune systems, but doggy familiars can be utilized magically for healing in these circumstances. In the Greek hospitals of the god Asclepius, dogs were encouraged to appear in patient dreams with healing instructions. The goddess Hecate is the quintessential dog goddess, but dogs are also linked with Artemis/Diana and the childbirth goddess Eileithyia. In medieval France women prayed to the dog saint Guinefort for safety in childbirth and healthy infants. The Egyptian dog deity is Anubis, like many dog gods, a funerary deity. The dog can be invoked for patients near death to ease transition.

The **mouse** probably got his reputation as a healing panacea because the mouse is the oldest known manifestation of the god Apollo, who became the great healer in Classical times. Even so, there are a few healing applications that are particularly linked to the mouse. One is fertility, an association which is easy to understand since mouse populations can explode quickly. Another is protection against infectious diseases, which again extends logically from our knowledge that mice are vectors for a number of diseases. The most persistent mouse remedy in folklore has been in connection with complaints of the urinary system, particularly bedwetting. Mice have also been used to treat diabetes, which is probably related to mouse associations with the urinary tract, since the salient symptom of diabetes is sweet smelling urine.

The **owl** is associated with good eyesight, especially night vision, due to her large eyes and nighttime habits. She is also linked with mental clarity, exemplified in the brilliant Greek owl goddess Athena. The most common owl remedy I have found, surprisingly, is for alcoholism and hangovers. The haggard owl-eyed look dehydrated people have after a night of drinking inspired this sympathetic medicine. Probably, if you resort to this remedy often enough you absorb some of Athena's wisdom and decide to embrace sobriety. The poorly understood phenomenon we call "crib death" was once attributed to the owl as death goddess taking back her children, and she was propitiated with charms to prevent this. Ishtar is the Mesopotamian owl goddess, and owl charms were used to promote maternal health and aid childbirth.

The **pig** (or boar) is the most important animal in pre-Christian Celtic art after the cow. The Welsh goddess Cerridwyn is generally believed to be a sow goddess, although Christian persecution related to the sow was especially harsh and effectively obliterated most references to the sacred aspects of this animal. Christian animus toward the sow probably began with the rivalry between early Greek Christians and initiates in the Eleusinian mysteries. The goddess Demeter, a sow goddess, was a central figure in the Eleusinian rites. The boar is also prevalent in Germanic pre-Christian art and is associated with the goddess Freya and her brother Freyr. The ancient Egyptian goddess Nut is a sow goddess. The sow goddess seems to have risen to prominence in early Neolithic societies because pigs thrived on cereals and were well integrated into agricultural practices. Even as ancient Egypt moved away from pork consumption for hygienic reasons as the Nile Valley became crowded, sow charms, spells, and amulets remained popular. The sow has traditionally been invoked for fertility. The presence of sows in funerary art suggests that the sow was also invoked when death was near.

Scorpion healing magic largely comes from Egypt and Mesopotamia and not surprisingly is focused on curing scorpion stings. The scorpion appears in preventative medicine in both of these cultures, especially for promoting healthy children. The scorpion is used to counter respiratory distress, fevers, and headaches, since these are symptoms of scorpion venom. The Egyptian scorpion goddess is Selket, although Isis is also invoked in association with scorpion medicine. In Mesopotamia the scorpion goddess was absorbed with other goddesses far in prehistory, but the Semitic goddesses Ishara and Ishtar are deities proficient in scorpion medicine.

Aside from the obvious use of **snakes** in addressing venomous snake bites, the snake is used in cases of chronic fatigue in adults or failure to thrive in infants. The snake ally is the first line of defense in listlessness of mysterious origin without other prominent symptoms. Snakes have been used as aphrodisiacs and for curing impotence. The Greek goddess Medusa is courted by many who work with snake medicine. Wadjet is a popular Egyptian snake goddess. Snakes were used in ancient Mediterranean societies to attract healing messages in dreams. Some snakes contain anti-inflammatory compounds, and there is a Chinese water snake that has been particularly useful in inflammatory diseases. This is the origin of the "snake oil" label for fraudulent medical practices: medical people in the American West learned about the healing properties of the water snake from Chinese immigrants and began prescribing extracts from indigenous North American snakes which were ineffective. Snakes were associated with medical fraud even earlier in Britain through the promulgation of "adder beads," supposedly formed from the solidified drool of adders. While adder beads may have been effective in spells invoking snake allies, many people bought the beads believing they actually came from adders. Social commentators from the Enlightenment lampooned possessors of adder beads similar to the way medical doctors in America would later inveigh against "snake oil salesmen." The snake is an effective healer but a deceptive healer. Move on to other spells and allies if the snake isn't helping and don't over-rely on this very powerful healer.

The **spider** is invoked for ailments involving movement because people bitten by spiders supposedly become agitated and "dance." The spider dance, known as the Tarantella in Italian, may have remote origins, but it became popular in the late Middle Ages, with the epicenter of the renewed craze in the German province of Saxony. Medical experts of the time believed the disease tarantism might or might not have an incendiary spider bite, but that it was characterized by burning sensations in the limbs and mental agitation similar to arachnid toxicity. While Christian authorities frowned on dancing, exceptions were made for people suffering from tarantism and for those helping the afflicted to "dance" away the toxins. The connection between Christian proscriptions against dancing and widespread occurrences of mental illness during the witch persecutions has not, to my knowledge, been explored, but an outbreak of hysteria among teenage girls in the Puritan community of Salem Massachusetts (and subsequent witch craze) occurred in the context of prohibitions on dancing. Invoke the spider to dissipate the effects of a toxic spider bite or to decrease agitation.

The **toad** is ubiquitous in European folklore for a wide array of ailments. Toad skin has antibacterial properties, so it was often used to fight infectious diseases. During the plague some people even tied dead toads under their armpits or stuck them in their pants to transfer antibacterial agents to the lymph nodes. Obviously the use of dead toads in medicine is messy and inconvenient, so the use of toads in healing spells flourished. Toads were also used to increase fertility, stimulate sexual desire, regulate menses, and aid childbirth. The toad was the treatment of choice for a wide variety of female reproductive ailments. Toads were commonly used for water retention, kidney stones, skin diseases, and excessive bleeding. Ointments containing toad venom, which has hallucinogenic properties, were used to aid shamanic journeying. Toads survived in fairy tales, though often maligned, but we don't have a lot of information about toad goddesses. The Lithuanian shape-shifting goddess Ragana can be depicted as a toad, which may be her primary aspect. The goddess Hecate acquired a toad aspect in late antiquity from the similarity between her name and that of the obscure Egyptian frog goddess Hekat. I believe that the Sheela Na Gig figure on medieval churches is a representation of a toad goddess. My rationale for this is elaborated in my book *Invoking Animal Magic*.

Weasels act as advisors to shamans, issuing healing prescriptions. In one Norse tale, the hero learns about a healing herb from watching weasels. In Europe, Asia, and North America weasels are either respected or reviled, often depending on the culture's attitude toward their indigenous healing traditions. They are considered powerful magical animals in many disparate cultures. I find the link between witchcraft and weasel somewhat mystifying. Perhaps it has to do with weasels in cold climates becoming white in winter, making them shape-shifters. Alternatively, it may be related to the weasel's ability to "go to ground" and hide quickly. These animals only show themselves when they want to.

The planet Mars is said to rule dentistry, which may be an association borrowed from the god Mars, a **woodpecker** god. Woodpeckers have strong beaks that they pound into wood in search of insects.

This is only a partial list of the healing powers of the animals above, and there are many others.

A question that sometimes comes up when invoking animals for healing is, what are the animals getting from this? When summoned on a spirit plane, animals engage willingly and non-coercively. The sincerity and good intentions with which you approach animal healers is what elicits their helpful response. Still, it is a shamanic principle to acknowledge help and reward it.

This is not payment but gift. Your gift may be a physical offering (a carrot on the altar for a deer) or a metaphysical offering (a gold coin given during a spirit journey). Gifts are what keep good energy flowing. Healing from animals is a gift to you.

British Shamanism

Elen Sentier

What is British shamanism?

Britain has been overrun and "civilized" by so many peoples and cultures over the past 2,000 years, from Christianity to the Norman Conquest, that nowadays people have forgotten that we have our own ancient ways here in Britain. The oldest drawing of our reindeer goddess which archaeology has (so far) found is 14,000 years old – that's well before the end of the last Ice Age. That drawing is in Cathole Cave, in SW Wales, and was only discovered in 2011. I suspect there's a lot more for us to find over the coming years which will affirm to those who didn't know about us that our old ways are indeed very ancient. And, nowadays, more and more people want to know about them.

The old ways have been handed down over the past twenty centuries through families and villages and they're a lot older than that, probably as old as humanity. They're not exclusive to those families. When someone with no history (that they know of) hears and wants to become part of us, we're open to them and will teach the old ways; thus we extend the knowing of them and, slowly, bring them back to everyday life.

Once you begin to look, and to make connections, you find them all over the place. For instance, the place-name Helen, or sometimes still Elen, litters maps of Britain, north, south, east and west; it refers to the name of the reindeer goddess, Elen of the Ways, whose drawing is in Cathole Cave. Once upon a time, reindeer ran here in Britain, up to 800 years ago, and they're back again in the Cairngorms, in the Highlands of Scotland. Britain was once a part of the Boreal Forest, that huge biome that cloaks the northern shoulders of Planet Earth from the tundra down to latitude 50° – or it did before humans began cutting it all down.

It's still the largest forest biome on the planet although reduced to perhaps half the size it was 10,000 years ago. Reindeer still roam in the wilderness bits of it we've left. So do the deer-folk who run with them, like the Caribou Folk of North America, the Sami people in Finland, and the Deer Folk of the region around Mongolia.

We here in Britain, our ancestors, were once part of this huge clan – for latitude 50° is the southern tip of Cornwall.

The ways of the deer folk, following the deer trods, still come down to us today even though there are no longer reindeer to teach us. We do have other deer though, particularly the great Red Deer of Scotland, Dartmoor, and Exmoor where I grew up; and the little Roe Deer, our other remaining native species, who you find hiding in woodland all over Britain. Our ways come from following the deer. Deer are a strongly migratory species, they carry in their genes and their inner knowing, in their essence, the wisdom of the summer and winter pastures, the kenning of the weather and the season-changes, the knowing of what is good to eat and what is not, of where water is, and how to find food under the snow. They know all this because they're deeply and completely attuned to the Earth, unlike our poor modern farm animals who live such a wretched and confused life they've mostly lost the plot. And so, indeed, have we humans! People nowadays are often afraid of nature, of weather, of wild places – do you know, I was once asked on a bushcraft weekend if badgers would eat you? While it was immediately funny, it was also horrific ... that there are people out there, nowadays, who truly don't know, and are afraid. That's being completely disconnected.

Being connected is what our old ways are about. Being connected with all the four elements of earth, water, fire and air, and the natural realms that they represent, those of rock and soil, rivers and seas, animals (including ourselves), and birds and insects. Our ancestors who followed the literal deer trods, as well as the spirit-ways of the deer, were connected to all that. On a very practical note, they wouldn't have survived if they hadn't been. You need to know all the other kingdoms of nature when you're personally dependent on them to provide your food, shelter, clothing, tools, everything you need to live. Even as short a time ago as when I was growing up, in the 1950s, people were far more connected to nature than they are now. And, the people I grew up with, including my family, were all very well aware of and connected to what we call otherworld, the spirit-life of Mother Earth. We knew to ask otherworld to help us live, help us have food and shelter ... and we knew, too, that everything is always exchange. We give to otherworld and they give to us. I grew up knowing this, and knowing how both to ask and to listen to the spirit-world, otherworld.

Let's take an example ... Dad used to shoot-for-the-pot, we got quite a lot of our meat this way, rabbits and hares, birds, venison. While Dad was proud of his marksmanship he didn't shoot "for fun" but to provide some of the food for the family. Before he went out, each time, he had a little ritual where he asked otherworld to give him some food, animals to shoot for the pot; sometimes it would be deer he asked for, sometimes pigeons or pheasants, at others a couple of rabbits. He would put together a pot of garden soil, another of water from our spring, a vase of flowers or leaves, and a candle, then he'd spend a few moments quiet, asking and listening to otherworld's response. Sometimes, when he'd asked for a deer he might be told that, at the moment, what he could have was a brace of rabbits. He'd always agree, he knew he'd get nothing at all if he didn't. Then he'd go out, go and lie-up somewhere and wait for the animals to come past him, and I'd often go with him, even as a little child I knew where my food came from. The deer would come past, and his animal, the one gifted him by otherworld, would stop and sometimes look at him, enabling him to take a good, quick, kill-shot. He'd only ever take the one, the one we needed right then, never be greedy.

Then we'd cut the animal up, pouch it as they call it, taking the guts and things we didn't want to eat and leaving them for the foxes and stoats, and the scavenger birds like the corvids, who would be grateful for the food to feed their own children. If we'd gone out after a red deer Dad would have a couple of my uncles along – red deer are huge, one man can't manage them on his own. We'd make a quick travois (sledge from tree-branches and a tarpaulin) and pull the deer back down to the Land Rover, load him up and take him home. Once home he'd be gralloched, unmade as we say in Britain, butchered into good cuts, with some for stew, and for the dogs and cats, as well as the roasting meat. A red deer would also be shared amongst two or three families as well, and likely some of it would be smoked to keep longer as freezers were certainly not common amongst 1950s country folk.

And then there'd be a thanking ceremony, short and brief and certainly not pompous, at which we would all offer a drop of blood, a finger-pricking, and reaffirm that we would care for the woods and the land, keep it good for the wild animals as well as for ourselves and the farm.

Our old ways are about sharing. Sharing with all the non-human world. We share with what is *not-us* even before we share with fellow humans and family. Everything on Earth is older than humans; they're all our elder brethren from whom we learn, so we gift back what we can in return for what is given to us. We share.

Our rites and rituals are focused on what we're doing, like giving thanks, or asking for the food in the first place. They're not about dancing round with mead and rose petals, or other rites that are really about making the humans feel good. They're about connecting, and connection; about being aware of all the rest of creation beyond yourself ... and knowing yourself to be a part of that.

I've known all of this for as long as I've been alive. My parents didn't wait until I was old enough – whenever would that be in any case? I went with them to the midwinter, midsummer celebrations on the local hilltop; and all the other festivals too. It was "what you did" and so it was "normal" for me. There were lots of Christians in the village as well as us pagans, and agnostics and atheists too, and while there were some prissy folk who wouldn't mix they were very few and far between. Our vicar was very good at this, he always joined in with things like blessing the plough harness for the first spring ploughing – we still ploughed with horses when I was a small child. And with burying the Lammas corn dolly in the first furrow ploughed the following February as earnest to the goddess for a good harvest. Later, when we'd moved on for a short time to ploughing using two traction engines to pull the plough across the field, we took the ceremonies across from the horses to the engines, and finally to the tractors. We knew that every part of each of them was made of Earth-Stuff – the horses, the brasses on the leather harness, the metal in the traction engines and later the tractors, all made of Earth-Stuff, so we thanked and celebrated it all.

When you grow up that way, learning that a tractor and horse are both made of the same very basic atoms, it really helps you feel your connectedness with everything, right in your bones ... for your bones, too, are made of atoms which might once have been a horse, or even a tractor.

It's an incredibly fundamental thing, feeling and knowing this connection. When you have it, you look at the whole of Life, the Universe and Everything in a very different way to the poor folk who believe everything is separate. You don't fear in the same way, and so you don't hate in the same way. You know that, one day, your body will die and all your atoms will go back into the huge Earth-Cauldron to become part of someone or something else, maybe lots of someones and somethings. You know that when you eat a cabbage, that cabbage becomes part of you; that when you pee and defecate it then goes on to become part of something else … maybe even another cabbage you will eat.

The old song, On Ilkla Moor Baht 'At, says it beautifully – go look up the words.

I also learned a lot from my Uncle Jack about wild animals, and how they will come to you. From when I was about 3 years old he would take me out in the woods at night to sit under a tree. We sat very still, and I learnt this quickly for Uncle Jack would say, "If you're not still and quiet no animals will come to you. Do you want them to come?" and I would nod, "then sit quiet and still," he'd tell me again. Nowadays people often say children cannot sit still, but they can if they're taught and if they know why, really why, it's a good thing to do. I learnt then and I still do it now. Quiet and still and all the night-denizens of the wood will come round you, and the day creatures too if you sit still and don't fidget. I was watching the moorhen and her chicks this morning, on our pond here, sitting still, not moving, not making a noise, and so she let me see lots of her family life with her chicks. Ask wildlife photographers, they know.

Watching non-human life shows you so much. It opens your mind, you no longer think of animals or plants as "it," nor do you make the crass assumption that they're "dumb animals." In fact, you're often staggered at the complexity of their relationships, and the skill with which animals work. Once you know this stuff in your bones your life changes. You really see them as your elder brothers, and your teachers … and all the shaman traditions know this. Our old ways here in Britain know it too.

How do you get this, how do you learn it? Practice, practice and yet more practice, until it's all in your autopilot, until it's what you do. But there's one big thing you have to do very first of all and that's get your head out of the way!

Modern life teaches us to revere the brain, the mind, thinking. We almost bow down to people who have alphabet soup after their names, we do what they say unquestioningly, and that's how to fall flat on your face (or the other bit!) in the old ways. Thinking is just one of the four functions (to use Jung's term), and these four functions relate to those four elements I spoke of earlier – earth, water, fire and air. But modern life has made thinking the god, the be-all and end-all of everything. It denigrates intuition and instinct, calls them "animal" meaning rubbish and useless. It puts feelings on a similar level. But thinking ... ahhhh, there's the Mount Olympus summit of all ambition. No wonder we make such a shocking mess of our own lives, our children's and all the rest of Life on Earth too. But we don't have to be like this. We can be really brave and go hunting and stalking for our own old ways, learn to live with the natural world and so, gradually, with the spirit-world too. We can get out of our heads and back into our instincts, feelings and intuition again. The old ways of Britain, like the old ways in every land, will lead you there, if you follow the deer trods.

So ... what's it all about?

Our basic principles, in the British old ways, are:

- Asking
- Listening
- Hearing
- Sharing
- Caring
- Being at-one with everything else in the Cosmos

Sounds really simple ... as my Dad use to say, it sounds simple but nobody said it was easy!

In fact, it's really hard because you have to un-learn so many habits you've had for the whole of your life. I was lucky, I was born into a family where the old ways had been practiced for countless generations so my un-learning was very small. But this just ain't the case for most people. Add in that they likely haven't begun to try learning the old ways until they're forty-something so that's forty-odd years of habits to unlearn. Hard work, like I said.

But don't get despondent, it can be done and I know lots of people who've done it. I teach students myself and I'm by no means the only one who does. You will have to go hunt for us though and then we'll likely test you to see if what we have really is what you want. Beginning the path of walking the deer trods isn't like going on a weekend course, no sort of holiday, and you can't put it away in the cupboard for the working week to bring it out again at the weekends. It permeates every atom of your life, and your relationships, so we old ones push hard to make sure you know this as best you can, and really do want to do it.

The best thing to do, if you want to do it, is to find yourself a place to sit quiet and still, a place you love, and try a daydream. Begin by saying, just the once, "Please show me the way to the teacher I need." It's as simple as that. Then you daydream, remember what you see, words said, images, phrases, and when you come back from your daydream sit quiet a while longer and ponder on it all. Draw and doodle things from your daydream, so they'll remind you later when you get back home. Then be very aware, watch and listen to all that happens around you and to you because otherworld will bring your wish to life ... but it just may not look how your head thinks it should! That's getting your head out of the way again. We're so used to doing what our head says we're blind to the rest of reality around us. But you can do it, if you want to.

The old ways of Britain lead you into life, into real reality rather than TV adverts showing a Hollywood version of life. They help you connect fully and contentedly with all of nature, and with all of otherworld, the spirit-world which is always there, all the time, but we mostly refuse to see it.

You can climb out of your box. You can find the old, old ways that connect you to Life, the Universe and Everything ... and you don't need white mice, or 42, or your towel or beer-n-peanuts, or the Hitchhiker's Guide to the Galaxy. And there won't be Vogons to shout at you or bore you to death with their poetry either LOL.

Otherworld will be delighted if you'd like to join in with the old ways of Britain. Anyone want to have a go?

Shamanic Story Weaving

Taz Thornton

Shamanism. As I write this, it's fair to say that all things "shamanic" have been gaining in popularity when it comes to the mind, body, spirit movement. Trouble is, the essence of shamanism is being somewhat lost in the process.

It's not uncommon to find people calling all kinds of practices "shamanic" simply because they include drumming, wafting around a bit of sage smoke or working with animal spirits. I've heard all kinds of tales about so-called shamanic work that are just about as far removed from shamanism as I can imagine.

Given the power-full (hyphen deliberate) potential of working shamanically, it's perhaps not surprising that so many are trying to tap into the energy. I've spent years learning about energy and spirit – as well as personal development – and it's fair to say that some of the shamanic tools I've learned knock spots off anything else (including some of the more left-brain self-improvement tools out there).

Trouble is, the shamanic threads of our own past in these British lands we tread have been so heavily eroded, it's difficult to find anything solid to hold onto and learn from. Furthermore, we could argue until the unicorns come home over whether the British Isles had any shamanic heritage in the first place. It's easy to fall into the blissful belief that every indigenous culture across the globe has some kind of shamanic heritage, though it's far more likely that most have at least some basis in animism … which is at the center of shamanic culture, but isn't shamanism per se.

When it comes to the UK, our pre-Roman spiritual past can be difficult to quantify, and that might be why so many who feel called towards shamanism either grasp at straws in terms of practical application, or eagerly swipe their credit cards to explore far-flung climes where people believe shamanic practice to be far more tangible.

Very often, if I'm talking to a group of people who are interested in shamanism, they'll cite all kinds of places and cultures they believe to be "shamanic." Most commonly, I'll hear people talk about the Americas, with a far smaller smattering of mentions for Tibet, Siberia, Mongolia and Australia. This really isn't the chapter for a history lesson on the origins of shamanism – and there's already plenty of debate and discussion about this point online – but it does go some way to explaining why these Celtic lands are oft ignored when it comes to working shamanically; generally speaking, when people feel that call, they rarely imagine they might be able to learn about, or develop, a shamanic skillset, on their British home soil.

Regardless of whether we choose to believe the ancient people of the British Isles had a shamanic culture (and I like to believe we did), there is nothing to stop us practicing shamanism on our home turf. Arguably, what sets shamanism aside from many other areas of spirituality is the journey work – where, usually to a drum beat, our energy body travels to the other realms to bring back teachings, healings and messages – and, in my experience, the spirits of these lands respond very well.

Of course, what also draws people to want to "shamanize" in other parts of the world are their perceptions of "better" or "more exotic" spirits to work with. There are, of course, a few lessons in ego to be aware of here, but that's for another book on another day. Parking that train of thought for a moment, let's just remember that while some might want to ally themselves with other climes to legitimize their want to work with wolf, bear or eagle spirits, those four-legged guides also used to travel our own lands at one time and eagle is most certainly still present. And if you're drawn to working with the fae and all things mystical ... psst ... come closer ... we have dragons!

Dragons, dryads, the faerie kingdom and queendom and all kinds of mystical beings – the stuff our "fairytales" are made from, and that brings me to the very heart of this chapter.

Shamanism and Storyweaving

It would be easy, at this point, to spin off into a fascinating discussion over whether those enchanting stories of old were ever really works of fiction at all. Some people theorize that those ancient tales from other parts of Europe were really a way to hide some of our old teachings, so they might survive the passage of time, the coming of the Church and those days when our old ways were being outlawed. There are all kinds of theories out there about the real origins of Easter egg hunts and the Easter bunny too, and how those traditions might have been morphed into their present day incarnations from so-called pagan traditions of old.

Regardless of whether there are truths woven between the words, many of these quirky, old stories are jam packed with beautiful teachings, and it's my belief that there are plenty of other wonderful stories being held safely by the guardians of Albion. Later in the chapter, I'll tell you exactly why I believe this and how – if you feel so inclined – you might be able to use shamanic journey work – and sometimes meditation – to channel some of those tales for your own loved ones.

Teaching stories, of course, have been used in cultures all over the world. For many years, I've been fascinated by them. Fables, legends, parables, myths ... whatever term is used, they're often full of rich lessons if we only search for them.

One of the greatest teachers on my spiritual path loved relaying these teaching tales from his time learning direct from elders in the Americas – stories of how Raven stole the sun, Jumping Mouse and many others became a high point of our workshops, as we gathered around the fire, eager to listen and learn. I'll always remember him explaining how the wise people of the village would tell these stories to groups of children, and how the messages always hit exactly where they needed to; he called this "shooting" someone with a story.

Since then, I've come across many wonderful storytellers, yet none seemed to be telling the stories of our own lands. Those European "fairytales" aside, what about stories from our own ancient past? What of our own beautiful tapestry? What of all those beautiful teachings held by the ancestors of our own lands?

It was after listening, enthralled, to a wonderful bard that I really felt the pull from Spirit to delve further, using many of the shamanic tools I hold dear. I felt the ancestor spirits tugging at my sleeve – and at my heart – to quest for our own parables ... and that's where my real adventure began.

It started with the land – for the lands we tread hold the bones and the teeth of the ancestors; through a series of meditations and shamanic journeys, I began to be gifted with some of the most beautifully-woven tales I'd ever heard. Later, working with some of my shamanism students, we widened the project, all connecting with the spirits of times past and all channeling amazing life lessons, told through wonderful stories. Clearly, the ancestors were pleased that finally, after hundreds of years, new story weavers were stepping forward, respectfully and with open hearts, to carry these teachings to new generations.

What I've found most amazing is that, despite the apparent age of these tales, their teachings are perfect for modern day. There are still plenty to be sourced and, for those who are practicing shamanism and interested in using those tools to tap into the magic of these lands, it seems the old ones are only too willing to pass their stories on to be carried into the future.

Answering the Call

There are many ways to get into the flow of storytelling and, for those of you wanting to go deeper into this body of work, I include plenty of ideas to help you connect with spirit to channel some beautiful tales in my first book, *Whispers from the Earth*.

If you can't wait to order a copy of *Whispers*, here are a few ideas about how to get started.

Like any exercise, it's always good to begin with a warm up, and storyweaving is no different – we need to start toning our "bardic muscles" with some gentle introductory work. In this way, we can encourage our creativity to flow and not get stuck trying to force a story onto the page, which simply creates a head/heart disconnect. Heart, you see, is far more important than head in storyweaving – we're not trying to invent teaching tales to fit a particular subject, as one might use isomorphic metaphors in NLP practices but, rather, allowing the words to flow through us, bringing all kinds of teachings with them as they grow. Sometimes, when channeling a story, the teachings are immediately obvious but, in many cases, I've re-read a channeled story years later and discovered a whole batch of new teachings; they really do deliver to us precisely what we need at the time – even if we weren't aware of our requirement!

So, how might we get into the flow of storyweaving? Well, one way might be to begin with something familiar to us and tap into our creativity to breathe new life into it. Allow yourself to think back to your favorite childhood fairytale, whatever that might be, and try to remember what so enthralled you about it. Looking back now, through the eyes of an adult, what teachings did it hold for you, and how might you be able to retell that story?

How My Story Began

Some years ago, I had the pleasure of meeting Canadian storyteller and harpist Jeff Stockton at a gathering. Jeff enthralled us all with a beautiful Celtic tale, before inviting us all to work in groups, retelling familiar stories to each other to bring forth their teachings. Sitting out in the sunshine that day, I listened to a retelling of Rumpelstiltskin and the Tale of Taliesin; I chose to tell the old story of the two wolves (there are lots of arguments over the etymology of this particular tale, but it carries a lovely message regardless).

As I wove together the words, creating the powerful teaching that had once hit me right between the eyes, it became evident that neither of my friends had heard the story before, and the power of the retelling suddenly filled my gut. You see, the thing about teaching stories is that they carry many lessons; often, the subtler teachings are hidden deep, deftly woven between the words, yet always finding their prey and pouncing, their lessons carrying deep into the soul of the eager listener.

Whichever teaching an individual needs is heard and absorbed right into the heart – that's why my old shamanic teacher used to refer to "shooting" people with a story. Until then, however, I'd never told a traditional teaching story to people who hadn't heard it before. I watched the emotions play out on their faces as the story unfurled, saw the teachings hit their mark, noticed their smiles as they began to understand.

It was after that experience that I began to wonder, in earnest, what happened to the teaching stories of these lands. Surely, we must have used them? I wondered if we might ever be able to get them back, or whether they'd been lost forever. It was then that I began to hear that whisper on the breeze, feel that familiar tug on my heart that would only become stronger if I tried to resist. It called my name, and I knew exactly who the words belonged to … this particular ancestor spirit has never pulled any punches with me. What she wants, she generally gets, and this was to be no exception.

"There are plenty more where this came from," came the voice, "we're holding them for you. The stories from your own lands. We hid them. We're waiting to share them again …" and then, as if by magic, the hidden teachings meant for my heart began to make sense; I realized little clues had been slipped into conversations throughout the day, I remembered some of the signs I'd seen in nature and how they all carried their own stories, and the idea for *Whispers from the Earth* began to take shape.

Just moments earlier, chatting with my storytelling pals, we'd touched on those teachings from our own lands being hidden in fairytales, put there to keep them safe when our own indigenous spirituality was being stamped out. We'd chatted about myths and legends, about the glimpses of our ancient spirituality still visible in things we take for granted. I remembered a fascination with the Brothers Grimm as a child, Hans Christian Andersen ... could these tales really carry glimpses of the truth, an essence of our neighboring cultures' past?

What of the stories from ancient Britain? Where were they? I began to scratch the surface with my shamanic work and asked my own trusted guides what happened in our lands. Did we have teaching stories? Might the spirits of our ancestors and the energies of the lands, the treefolk and the rock people be holding onto "Ye Olde British Teaching Stories"? I wanted to hear them now, wanted to learn, to explore. The answer, from that oh-so-familiar voice, dropped into my head and heart again almost immediately; there was that whisper again, deep within my chest: "They're here. We have them. We're waiting ..."

Continuing the Story

From that point, shamanic storyweaving became a regular part of my work; sometimes I'd journey at home, or in a quiet location, sometimes I'd go out into nature, listening to my guides and taking their instruction over where to sit, tune in and ask for a story. Each time, without fail, a beautifully complete tale was gifted to me.

In the essence of fairness, I should point out that I'm a writer by trade – I spent years as a journalist and editor before following my calling to work with spirit and to help people tap into their truth and personal power.

Just in case you're thinking it should be easy for me to just rustle up a quick story using my imagination, let me tell you where that theory falls down! Anyone who writes for a living will tell you about the editing process, the writers' block, the fits and starts, the lack of self-belief that so often comes with the job and so on. Using shamanic work to quest for stories was a completely different experience: either the story was narrated to me and I was able to write everything I'd been told, or I was shown the story playing out in full, glorious technicolor. There was no editing. No having to piece the sentences together in the hope of "jigsawing" a story. No gaps to fill. These stories were given whole, without the need to tap into my brain-based imagination banks. In fact, these stories were given to me so beautifully and completely that sometimes I feel like a bit of a fraud for having my name on the cover of *Whispers from the Earth*. Sure, I authored the introduction, explained a little about channeling stories and shared some advice for people wanting to use similar techniques but, for the stories themselves, I was absolutely the hollow bone – merely the conduit for the tales to pass through.

When I asked some of my shamanic students if they'd like to try using the same techniques, they had precisely the same levels of success, and only a couple of them were professional writers!

Could this Be Real?

Whether you choose to believe shamanism really has enabled me to tap into some of those wonderful teaching stories of times past is entirely up to you. Honestly, if you'd rather think I – and my students – have merely been gifted with wondrously creative imaginations, it absolutely is no skin off my nose. What's important is that the stories are carried forward and continue to work their healings and transformations for the people who need them, as they have been doing so far.

In fact, when I sell a copy of *Whispers* in person, I sometimes hand it over with the caveat that people may skip the first couple of chapters and go straight to the stories if they choose; it can be either a manual to help people get started with channeling and questing for their own stories, or simply treated as a fantastical story book for grown-ups.

I know what I believe. I know what the people who've used shamanic journeying work in this way believe. The rest is up to you.

In the words of Roald Dahl: "Those who don't believe in magic will never find it."

Contributors

Dorothy Abrams is the co-founder of the Web PATH Center, a pagan church and teaching facility in Lyons, New York, USA. She is the author of *Identity and the Quartered Circle: Studies in Applied Wicca* and editor of *Sacred Sex and Magick* by the Web PATH Center.

Elen Sentier grew up in the old ways of Britain through her family and the elders of the villages where she lived. She is the author of a number of books including, *The Celtic Chakras, Elen of the Ways, Trees of the Goddess* and *Merlin: Once and Future Wizard.*

Hearth Moon Rising is a Dianic priestess and priestess of Ishtar in the Fellowship of Isis. She is the author of *Invoking Animal Magic: A guide for the pagan priestess* and *Divining with Animal Guides: Answers from the world at hand.* Hearth lives in the Adirondack Mountains of upstate New York where she pursues a nature-based practice. She blogs at hearthmoonrising.com.

Imelda Almqvist is a shamanic teacher and painter based in London, UK. She teaches courses in shamanism and sacred art internationally. She is the author of *Natural Born Shamans – A Spiritual Toolkit for Life.*

Julie Dollman is a Shamanic Healer who trained and graduated with the Four Winds Society back in 2005. She now works as a full-time shamanic practitioner in rural Ireland. She is the author of *Living Shamanism.*

Janet Gale is a Doctor of Metaphysical Science, shamanic practitioner and teacher, Usui and Karuna Reiki Master, energy healer, Acutonics Tuning Fork practitioner, celebrant, and certified yoga Instructor. She lives in Cochrane, Canada and is the author of *The Rush Hour Shaman*.

Jez Hughes is the founder of Second Sight Healing, established in 2005 and based in the UK, a center that offers a variety of accredited programs of Shamanic Training and initiation from basic workshops to intensive Practitioner levels. He also teaches around the UK and Europe and is the author of *The Heart of Life*.

Kenn Day is a professional shaman, with a private practice in Cincinnati, Ohio in the United States, where he lives with his beloved wife and daughter. He also passes on the teachings of post-tribal shamanism (a term he coined back in the late 1980s to describe his work) through his writings and workshop series offered around the United States. He is the author of *Dance of Stones: a Shamanic Road Trip* and *Post-Tribal Shamanism: a New Look at the Old Ways*. He is available for remote healing consults as well and can be reached via his website at www.shamanstouch.com

Laura Perry is a Pagan artist and storyteller with a special interest in the ancient Minoans and is the author of *Ariadne's Thread*. Laura teaches an online course in Minoan Paganism and has designed a Minoan-themed Tarot deck. www.LauraPerryAuthor.com

S. Kelley Harrell is a modern shaman, and author of *Gift of the Dreamtime*, and *Teen Spirit Guide to Modern Shamanism*. A lifelong intuitive, she has worked with a local and international client base since 2000. She holds a Masters degree in Religious Studies, and is an ordained interfaith minister. Her work is Nature-based, and honors the paths of animism, Seiðr, and Druidry. She works closely with the Elder Futhark Runes and divine Nature Spirits of eastern North Carolina. Her shamanic practice is *Soul Intent Arts*. Find *The Weekly Rune* on her blog, Intentional Insights, at soulintentarts.com

Taz Thornton is a shamanic healer, workshop leader and crafter of sacred ceremonial items, including rattles, medicine bags, dance staffs, medicine jewelry and the "Shaman Stones" personal guidance system. Taz offers training in shamanism and meditation, one-to-one healing, distance healing and group sessions, as well as space clearing services. She is the author of *Whispers from the Earth*. www.firechild-shamanism.co.uk

Moon Books

PAGANISM & SHAMANISM

What is Paganism? A religion, a spirituality, an alternative belief system, nature worship? You can find support for all these definitions (and many more) in dictionaries, encyclopaedias, and text books of religion, but subscribe to any one and the truth will evade you. Above all Paganism is a creative pursuit, an encounter with reality, an exploration of meaning and an expression of the soul. Druids, Heathens, Wiccans and others, all contribute their insights and literary riches to the Pagan tradition. Moon Books invites you to begin or to deepen your own encounter, right here, right now.

If you have enjoyed this book, why not tell other readers by posting a review on your preferred book site.

Recent bestsellers from Moon Books are:

Journey to the Dark Goddess
How to Return to Your Soul
Jane Meredith
Discover the powerful secrets of the Dark Goddess and
transform your depression, grief and pain into healing and
integration.
Paperback: 978-1-84694-677-6 ebook: 978-1-78099-223-5

Shamanic Reiki
Expanded Ways of Working with Universal Life Force Energy
Llyn Roberts, Robert Levy
Shamanism and Reiki are each powerful ways of healing; together,
their power multiplies. *Shamanic Reiki* introduces techniques to
help healers and Reiki practitioners tap ancient healing wisdom.
Paperback: 978-1-84694-037-8 ebook: 978-1-84694-650-9

Pagan Portals – The Awen Alone
Walking the Path of the Solitary Druid
Joanna van der Hoeven
An introductory guide for the solitary Druid, *The Awen Alone* will
accompany you as you explore, and seek out your own place
within the natural world.
Paperback: 978-1-78279-547-6 ebook: 978-1-78279-546-9

A Kitchen Witch's World of Magical Herbs & Plants
Rachel Patterson
A journey into the magical world of herbs and plants, filled with
magical uses, folklore, history and practical magic. By popular
writer, blogger and kitchen witch, Tansy Firedragon.
Paperback: 978-1-78279-621-3 ebook: 978-1-78279-620-6

Medicine for the Soul
The Complete Book of Shamanic Healing
Ross Heaven
All you will ever need to know about shamanic healing and how to
become your own shaman...
Paperback: 978-1-78099-419-2 ebook: 978-1-78099-420-8

Shaman Pathways – The Druid Shaman
Exploring the Celtic Otherworld
Danu Forest
A practical guide to Celtic shamanism with exercises and
techniques as well as traditional lore for exploring the Celtic
Otherworld.
Paperback: 978-1-78099-615-8 ebook: 978-1-78099-616-5

Traditional Witchcraft for the Woods and Forests
A Witch's Guide to the Woodland with Guided Meditations and
Pathworking
Melusine Draco
A Witch's guide to walking alone in the woods, with guided
meditations and pathworking.
Paperback: 978-1-84694-803-9 ebook: 978-1-84694-804-6

Wild Earth, Wild Soul
A Manual for an Ecstatic Culture
Bill Pfeiffer
Imagine a nature-based culture so alive and so connected,
spreading like wildfire. This book is the first flame...
Paperback: 978-1-78099-187-0 ebook: 978-1-78099-188-7

Naming the Goddess

Trevor Greenfield

Naming the Goddess is written by over eighty adherents and scholars of Goddess and Goddess Spirituality.

Paperback: 978-1-78279-476-9 ebook: 978-1-78279-475-2

Shapeshifting into Higher Consciousness

Heal and Transform Yourself and Our World with Ancient Shamanic and Modern Methods

Llyn Roberts

Ancient and modern methods that you can use every day to transform yourself and make a positive difference in the world.

Paperback: 978-1-84694-843-5 ebook: 978-1-84694-844-2

Readers of ebooks can buy or view any of these bestsellers by clicking on the live link in the title. Most titles are published in paperback and as an ebook. Paperbacks are available in traditional bookshops. Both print and ebook formats are available online.

Find more titles and sign up to our readers' newsletter at
http://www.johnhuntpublishing.com/paganism
Follow us on Facebook at https://www.facebook.com/MoonBooks
and Twitter at https://twitter.com/MoonBooksJHP